The Active
Classroom
Field Book

The Complete Active Classroom Series

The Active Classroom...

. . . provides practical strategies for shifting the role of students from passive observers to active participants in their own learning.

The Active Teacher...

. . . focuses on the critically important first five days of school and becoming a proactive rather than reactive teacher.

The Active Mentor...

. . . gives teacher mentors practical strategies for going beyond support to actively accelerating the growth of new teachers.

The Active Classroom Field Book...

. . . highlights practices inspired by the bestselling *The Active Classroom*—and shows how teachers shifted responsibility for learning from themselves to their students!

The Active Workshop...

. . . illustrates how workshop facilitators can accelerate the continuous-improvement of educators by turning attendees into active participants.

The Active Classroom Field Book

Success Stories
From the
Active
Classroom

Ron Nash

CORWIN
A SAGE Company

For information:

Corwin
A SAGE Company
2455 Teller Road
Thousand Oaks, California 91320
www.corwin.com

SAGE Ltd.
1 Oliver's Yard
55 City Road
London EC1Y 1SP
United Kingdom

SAGE Pvt. Ltd.
B 1/I 1 Mohan Cooperative
    Industrial Area
Mathura Road, New Delhi 110 044
India

SAGE Asia-Pacific Pte. Ltd.
33 Pekin Street #02-01
Far East Square
Singapore 048763

Printed in the United States of America

Library of Congress Cataloging-in-Publication Data

Nash, Ron J.
The active classroom field book : success stories from the active classroom / Ron Nash.
    p. cm.
Includes bibliographical references and index.
ISBN 978-1-4129-8132-3 (pbk.)
    1. Active learning—United States—Case studies. 2. Education, Elementary—United States—Case studies. I. Title.

LB1027.23.N36 2010
372.139—dc22   2010004990

This book is printed on acid-free paper.

10 11 12 13 14 10 9 8 7 6 5 4 3 2 1

Acquisitions Editor:	Hudson Perigo
Associate Editor:	Joanna Coelho
Editorial Assistant:	Allison Scott
Production Editor:	Veronica Stapleton
Copy Editor:	Adam Dunham
Typesetter:	C&M Digitals (P) Ltd.
Proofreader:	Dennis W. Webb
Indexer:	Molly Hall
Cover Designer:	Karine Hovsepian

Contents

Preface

It has long been my contention that many teachers who go home exhausted do so because they did most of the work during the course of the school day, while the students did too little and were engaged too infrequently. The opposite is true in the classrooms of the happiest and most well-adjusted teachers whom I have observed over the years. In those classrooms, the kids do more work than the teachers. In those classrooms, the teachers are process facilitators, while the students are in perpetual motion (figuratively and literally) and engaged in every way imaginable. The kids do the work; the kids enjoy coming to school; the kids talk *freely* at home about "what happened at school today" (what a concept!)—and the kids learn.

In my first classroom (1970s), I gave my ninth-grade students the benefit of my vast knowledge of U.S. history (four years of college in the making) in the form of some stellar lectures, using a marvelous piece of electronic technology called an overhead projector. I uncovered the notes on my transparencies one at a time, so that my students could concentrate on each piece of information separately. I often turned out half the overhead lights (so the students could see the screen), and then I elucidated, illustrated, gesticulated, pontificated, and otherwise entertained them for the better part of 45 minutes while they took copious notes and hung on my every word and gesture. Thus enlightened, they took their notebooks home and spent time each evening processing the information I had so generously provided. I was a veritable font of wisdom at the age of 23, come to think of it, and to this day I suspect my former students still talk about the "Nash lectures" in their truly reflective and nostalgic moments at class reunions.

Perhaps not.

When I began my teaching career, lecture and other forms of teacher talk predominated, and we as teachers functioned as important information givers. Other sources of readily available information came from print sources; the size of our school and community libraries limited the amount of resource materials available. Encyclopedias were rarely current, and interlibrary loan was the only way to get items not found in the school or local library. Print was *in,* and print was *it;* constantly keeping print resources up to date could get expensive. It might also take a reference librarian who knew how to conduct searches effectively to come up with what the erstwhile teacher or student needed for a term paper or thesis. Sources of information were relatively few compared to today, and teachers were critical contributors to the information pipeline.

By today's standards, the flow in that pipeline was a mere trickle. Today's students can get infinitely more information on George Washington with the click of a mouse than I could have provided *had I spent the entire school year teaching nothing but George Washington.* I Googled Ben Franklin recently and got almost seven million hits in .25 seconds. *Seven million hits.* Any teacher who believes his or her *primary* function is simply to deliver information on anything related to history or any other subject is in danger of missing the proverbial boat. Kids have more access to information about everything imaginable than anything dreamt of in our philosophy during the 1970s. Access is fast and free; it is *all* information *all* the time.

Teachers still deliver information, of course, because—let's face it—students don't necessarily spend much time Googling George Washington on their own. But a good deal of the modern teacher's task has shifted to helping students *make sense* of the information to which they have 24-hour access. Having discovered an article or entry on the Web, how can students then separate fact from fiction, opinion from fact, right from wrong, the correct from the incorrect . . . or the patently malicious? With all the words available in a cut-and-paste format, how do students learn how to arrange their own thoughts in ways that are fresh, original, and not plagiarized? Doing these things requires critical-thinking skills—and this is where teachers can be of immeasurable service.

In an age where many families struggle to survive, how can young people learn and master the skills necessary to make the right decisions and solve myriad life problems? At a time when communication skills are critical to global success in business, how do students learn to communicate effectively, orally and in writing? How do kids who have been weaned on staring at television and computer screens for hours on end learn to focus on another human being long enough to practice the art of active listening? How do children and adolescents who *don't* spend an hour at the dinner table having adult-facilitated conversations on many topics learn to explain, illustrate, summarize, clarify, apply, infer, analyze, and synthesize? Absent any other venue for the purpose, these skills must be developed in the classroom.

A student who is expected to do more than find the correct answer on a multiple choice test has to move up the cognitive ladder under the direction of teachers committed to getting students to share and analyze their thinking, come to conclusions based on their thinking—and *defend* those conclusions. Classrooms have to be active, engaging, intriguing, emotionally safe, and contemplative places where kids can take risks and make mistakes on the way to becoming educated, thoughtful, and *involved* citizens in adulthood. Students need to discover, practice, and sharpen the skills necessary to think critically and make the right decisions in life. Our future as a nation requires that students arrive at an intellectual place where they can create the innovations, services, and products of tomorrow's ever-more-global economy. Teachers are the chief facilitators of this process.

The road to this future for our children and our nation lies in the classrooms of today; this means teachers need to be aware of how the brain learns. Teachers need to read everything they can find on this topic; by doing so, they can see how movement, conversation, reflection, and collaboration affect retention and understanding. Administrators need to take note of the latest research that shows the connection between exercise and cognition (not to mention healthy bodies). Districts can help by *increasing* the amount of exercise kids get every day. Too many schools are reducing the time devoted to physical education and recess in a counterproductive effort to get students to "hunker down" and "concentrate." Brain cells need a steady supply of neurotransmitters (think dopamine, serotonin, and norepinephrine) in order to communicate with each other, and exercise releases those neurotransmitters (Smith, 2005, p. 136). Kids who move, play, talk, and laugh are in a better position to learn than those who sit for a 90-minute block, listening to the teacher talk.

Twenty-first–century educators need to acknowledge the massive changes taking place *outside* the classroom by changing what we do *inside* the classroom. One brief example: A student sits passively in a high school block while the teacher talks—then goes home to a digital world where images on a television screen follow each other at breakneck speed. In her bedroom, the student sits at a computer screen with several Web sites open at once, listening to music. A cell phone is on the desk, and instant messaging is at the ready in the corner of the screen. The student, who has at her beck and call a remote and a mouse, controls every bit of this. This represents total control of the pictures and the sound; one image replaces another in the blink of an eye, and the student's brain shifts its focus perhaps thousands of times in a typical evening at the computer. The next day, she will once again go to school and sit for 90 minutes at a desk, with one image—that of the teacher—in front of her. The contrast is stark, and the result is that the student may *prefer* home to school; she will most likely prefer rapidly shifting images to a single image; and she will appreciate the opportunity to get up and walk around when the spirit moves.

The purpose of this book is not to show teachers how to harness the power of electronic technology. Rather, it is an attempt to help teachers engage students through the use of inexpensive—but effective—brain-based strategies that encompass movement, collaboration, conversation, reflection, feedback, and the processing of information in order to accelerate a student's own continuous improvement journey. In the course of eight chapters, we'll explore these themes, and we'll add lessons, activities, and classroom vignettes contributed by the teachers listed in the Acknowledgments. The teachers whose classrooms we'll visit here have shifted their students from passive observers to active participants in their own learning.

Chapter 1: Squeeze Play

When I was a kid in Pennsylvania, we spent tons of time outdoors, playing kick the can, red rover come over, tag, and hide and seek. Winter brought snow football, snowball fights, and the construction of (if I do say so myself) some pretty elaborate snow forts. Unbeknownst to us at the time, that exercise contributed to not only our general health; it also helped develop our social and problem-solving skills, as we'll see later. In this first chapter, we'll explore the uses and benefits of movement and exercise in schools and classrooms.

Chapter 2: For Whom the (Dinner) Bell Tolls

As a Boomer growing up in the 1950s, dinner was an opportunity to talk and share ideas; it was a time to recap and analyze the day's events. The meal lasted almost an hour; it was billed in our neighborhood, at least, as a regularly scheduled—*and completely mandatory*—event. In this chapter, we'll talk about how this has changed and how that difference affects the teacher's role in developing the communication skills of students. We'll see that getting students to stand, pair, share, discuss, summarize, reflect, and otherwise process information goes a long way toward improving those important social skills.

Chapter 3: Setting the Table for Success

Outstanding teachers know that the first week of school is critical to the ultimate success of their students, no matter the grade level. Procedures that are practiced *until they become routine* contribute to the smooth running of any classroom. In classrooms where teachers jump into content before establishing some basic norms and processes, behavior and discipline problems may well multiply over time. We'll go inside classrooms where teachers put the process horse in front of the content cart.

Chapter 4: First One at the Bus Stop

Reflecting on hundreds of classroom visits over my time in education, I have come to the conclusion that when students enjoy coming to class, teachers will find the going easier than in cases where students are more or less dragged kicking and screaming into the classroom on a daily basis. One fifth grader contrasted her fourth-grade experience with what she was doing one year later; she told us she went from finding reasons to miss the school bus *to being the first one at the bus stop.* Same student. Different school environment. Different results. In this chapter, we'll explore the things kids love to do and experience in class.

Chapter 5: Feedback Pure and Simple

Expanding on a point made in the previous chapter—and based on the assumption that students rely on clear, consistent feedback in order to make adjustments and course changes in their own continuous-improvement journeys—we'll highlight ways to provide that feedback. Students need to know where they are now, where they *want* to go, and how to get there.

Chapter 6: When Teachers Tick and Classrooms Click

There may be many reasons why teachers love what they are doing, and teachers who love what they are doing give *students* one more reason to enjoy coming to school. Teachers whose students are successful as a result of their own efforts are happier in the profession . . . and more likely to stay in teaching. For some teachers, simply shifting kids from passive observers to *active classroom participants* is a seminal event in their own continuous-improvement journeys. On our own journey through this chapter, we'll look at teachers who tick and classrooms that click.

Chapter 7: Energize, Energize, Energize

I was in a classroom where the teacher played some upbeat music to transition the students from their seats to standing pairs; they "grooved" to their new locations, and she grooved right along with them. For the entire time I was in the classroom, I marveled at the energy she displayed in many ways; she modeled movement, humor, and storytelling; she demonstrated to them in every way that she loved what she did. This energy was highly infectious, and I spent my time in that classroom regretting I had to leave after 30 minutes. In this chapter, we'll visit classrooms that run an energy surplus.

Chapter 8: Reflecting on Reflection

Teachers who take the time to reflect on experience, either alone or collaboratively, put themselves in a better position to improve their own classroom performance. By contrast, teachers who use the same lessons year after year, and are satisfied with the status quo in their classrooms, are less likely to see improvement for themselves or their students. As we'll see, students can be part of the reflective process during the school year; their insights and perspectives can be informative and invaluable. In this final chapter, we'll explore ways to take advantage of the power of individual and collaborative reflection.

In the course of my four decades in education, I have noticed that the most effective *teachers* are those dedicated to continuous improvement in the classroom. The best *administrators* are those committed to continuous improvement in the building through the active and intentional support of instructional and support staff. The happiest and most well-adjusted *students* are those who feel safe in taking the risks necessary for improvement—satisfied that the adults in the building actively seek out and employ the strategies, tools, and techniques essential for that success. School communities with that kind of *can-do* and *will-do* attitude create a perfect storm of energy, engagement, and activity calculated to make students an integral part of their own continuous-improvement process.

Acknowledgments

This fourth volume in the *Active Classroom Series* is full of success stories, and I am grateful to those elementary-, middle-, and high-school teachers who allowed me to share their lessons, activities, and strategies. I have listed their names below, along with the name of an assistant professor and an outstanding Virginia elementary principal whose school is making excellent progress on the continuous-improvement highway.

Becky Bowerman, Elementary-School Teacher

Marylise Cobey, Elementary-School Teacher

Dani Crawford, Middle-School Teacher

Jenny Sue Flannagan, University Assistant Professor

Kathy Galford, Middle-School Teacher

Dana Hand, Elementary-School Teacher

Kathy Hwang, Elementary-School Principal

Emma Jeter, Elementary-School Teacher

Nikki Martel, Elementary-School Teacher

Stephanie Meister, Elementary-School Teacher

Julie Poclayko, High-School Teacher

Cindy Rickert, Elementary-School Teacher

Elizabeth Scheine, Elementary-School Teacher

Kelly Smith, Elementary-School Teacher

Gary Spedden, High-School Teacher

Yvonne Stroud, Middle-School Teacher

Deni Trombino, High-School Teacher

Art Truesdell, Upper-School Teacher

As always, I thank my editor at Corwin, Hudson Perigo, along with the rest of a strong and supportive Corwin team.

Finally, I thank my wife, Candy, for her continued support and encouragement.

About the Author

 **Ron Nash** is the author of the Corwin bestseller *The Active Classroom* (2008), along with *The Active Teacher* (2009) and *The Active Mentor* (2010). Nash's professional career in education has included teaching social studies at the middle- and high-school levels. He also served as an instructional coordinator and organizational development specialist for the Virginia Beach City Public Schools for 13 years. In that capacity, Nash conducted workshops and seminars for thousands of teachers, administrators, substitute teachers, and teacher assistants. In 2007, he founded Ron Nash and Associates, Inc., a company dedicated to helping teachers shift students from passive observers to active participants. Nash can be contacted at www.ronnashandassociates.com.e

To Jim, Steve, and Tim

Introduction

My first book, *The Active Classroom* (2008), was written to give teachers practical strategies for shifting kids from passive observers to active participants in their own learning. This was followed by *The Active Teacher* (2009), a book that emphasized the importance of planning and continuous improvement as twin accelerants of ultimate success for teachers. The third entry in this series, *The Active Mentor* (2010), highlighted the investments teacher mentors, administrators, peers, and support staff can make in order to keep new teachers from simply hanging it up and walking away after a few weeks, months, or years. All three books stress meaningful and frequent collaboration in classrooms, buildings, and districts—all in pursuit of continuous improvement and results.

This fourth entry in the *Active Classroom Series* is an opportunity to explore some favorite themes (movement, engagement, face-to-face student conversation, process improvement, and the importance of feedback, to name a few). It also gives me a chance to highlight some success stories from teachers who are using the active-classroom strategies. These examples are not formal lesson plans; they are, for the most part, short vignettes that demonstrate or underscore a concept or instructional strategy.

The entire *Active Classroom Series* is predicated on the belief that preparation, application, evaluation, and adjustment are all components in a continuous-improvement journey that ramps up instruction and student performance. The books in this series support the notion that, in order to make progress, students must be actively and consistently involved their own learning. By the same token, teachers can accelerate their own progress by involving themselves in collaborative improvement efforts at the building level. Principals and district administrators need to enlist the support of teacher leaders in creating self-evaluating improvement systems that can outlive them. Truly active teachers and administrators are constantly in motion in a way that contributes to student progress and systems improvement. Active teachers and administrators don't simply react to events as they occur; they take events into their hands and move classrooms, buildings, and districts relentlessly forward. This book will highlight teachers and administrators who have done just that.

1

Squeeze Play

Donnie was too quick, and I had strayed too far from the can. He had the shorter route to the tree; before I could react, he kicked the can across the graveled driveway and into the neighbor's yard. Donnie raised his hands in triumph and declared victory at the top of his lungs. The rest of the kids came running as they realized the game was over. As we all gathered under the huge oak tree, Donnie's mom came to the side door of his house to announce that it was time for dinner. As we all scattered to our own homes for the evening meal, someone retrieved the can from the yard next door and threw it under the oak tree, where it would remain until the neighborhood kids made it the centerpiece of yet another afternoon's fun and games . . . including kick the can.

When I was growing up in Pennsylvania in the 1950s, outdoor games like kick the can, red rover come over, hide and seek, tag, four square, and a dozen others occupied the kids in my neighborhood for hours on end. Twisted ankles, skinned knees, and broken bones were the widely accepted consequences of preadolescent years that were very much lived outside. We held neighborhood parades, spent hours in the creek that ran between properties at the end of the street, and chased each other through backyards up and down Gibson Street. One neighbor had a swimming pool and a small basketball court, and in good weather both were crowded. Winter storms did not deter us; we built snow forts and played snow football for hours on end. I can remember spending a great deal of time shivering and thawing out on a little chair over the living room register, sipping hot cocoa provided by my grandmother. We slept well at night because we had played well during the day.

I can remember the day my grandparents, with whom I spent my early youth, brought home their very first television set. It was a black and white TV—there were few color sets at the time—and my grandfather would watch the evening news and his beloved baseball; for my part, I discovered *The Mickey Mouse Club* and *The Howdy Doody Show.* These were pleasant diversions, but as kids, our time was spent outdoors. Walking home from school, I anticipated doing my homework (mandatory) and watching Annette, Cubby, and the rest of the Mickey Mouse Club gang before washing up and reporting to our kitchen for dinner (also mandatory). Then, it was outside again while it was still light enough to play and perhaps get into trouble (optional, but relatively frequent, as I recall). During any given week, I was outside far more often than I was in the house, and I watched perhaps five hours of television per week—most of that very early on Saturday mornings—before heading back outdoors.

We burned off calories by the ton, and obesity was a vocabulary word. Dinner was a regularly scheduled event, *and conversation with adults during mealtime was part of the deal.* During the summer vacation and on weekends, we came inside long enough to eat lunch—then it was back outside. Exercise and conversation were two sides of the coin of life in the fifties—at least for the kids in the two-dozen or so houses on my block. We enjoyed watching television, but the main event took place on a daily basis in the yards, creeks, streets, and alleys of my small hometown in northwestern Pennsylvania. It was rough and tumble; it was often highly competitive; and it was outdoors.

Smith (2005) emphasizes the importance of play in the lives of kids, pointing out that it is like "the best learning" in that "play involves lots of rehearsal and repetition" as "children do the same things again and again" (p. 160). To play kick the can in our neighborhood required three things:

1. We needed a can, of course. A new can was preferable, but one that was well battered, but functional, was acceptable.

2. We had to be *physically present* for the game. There were no "virtual" kick-the-can sessions; as long as we could assemble at least five neighborhood kids for that or any other outdoor pastime, we were ready to go.

3. In any number of different outdoor games, we would invariably agree on a set of rules, determine as a group if a rule had been broken, and subsequently—*and collaboratively*—work out any number of problems or sticky situations related to the game or activity.

We were active, and if inclement weather seemed likely, we put on our galoshes and raincoats, and we went outside anyway. The use of the family car for any purpose was limited; most of the kids in town walked to school. Smith (2005) recommends, in light of a reduction in the amount of outdoor exercise they get, we not lose sight of the value of play in the lives of children:

> With more and more children being delivered to and picked up from neighborhood schools, sitting in front of televisions or computer screens, and losing the skills of cooperative play their grandparents learned, maybe it is time to start teaching children to play. (p. 160)

Play that combines exercise with social interaction is healthy, and it enhances cognition.

Exercise and Cognition

Medina (2008) laments that in our headlong rush to pass end-of-year state tests, schools are squeezing physical education and recess out of the school day, thus reducing the amount of exercise students get in school. Medina affirms, "cutting off physical exercise—the very activity most likely to improve cognitive performance—to do better on a test score is like trying to gain weight by starving yourself" (p. 25). Ratey (2008) reminds us, "In today's technology-driven, plasma-screened-in world, it's easy to forget that we are born movers—animals, in fact—because we've engineered movement right out of our lives" (p. 3). When a kid today announces he is going to go play baseball, he may in fact mean he is headed for his bedroom and an individual session with a video game. A snowstorm was an invitation to go outdoors for snowball fights and snow football; how many kids today look out the window at the falling snow and think to themselves, "I hope we don't lose power."

If indeed there is a trend away from regular physical exercise on the part of children, this is doubly disturbing because the same physical exercise that has a positive effect on the health of our kids also improves cognition. Medina (2008) cites a study that found that kids who jogged for half an hour two or three times per week began to show improvement in cognitive performance 12 weeks into the study. According to Medina, "When the exercise program was withdrawn, the scores plummeted back to pre-jogging levels" (p. 15). Physical exercise is critically important for kids; it keeps them physically healthy while it enhances their ability to think.

In one Canadian study (Shephard, 1996, in Trost & van der Mars, 2009–2010), over 500 elementary students were given a full extra hour of PE *every day*. The result was that "students in grades two through six who received additional physical education earned better grades in French, mathematics, English, and science than did students who received the standard one period per week" (p. 62). When I present in schools around the country, I often have the PE teachers stand and be recognized. While they are standing, I explain that "these people are your first line of offense against obesity and lethargy, and they prepare your kids for their next stint in your classrooms by improving blood flow, increasing heart rate, and releasing neurotransmitters by the ton."

The clear connection between movement and cognition has implications for teachers. Movement, as we have seen, increases blood flow; that increased blood flow benefits the brain by carrying to it more glucose (for energy) and oxygen. Teachers who have their students sit for extended periods in an effort to help them concentrate are working at cross-purposes. If movement sends more blood to the brain, it follows that teachers should give students every opportunity to move in the classroom. Rather than squeeze physical education out of the curriculum, districts need to make certain kids get plenty of exercise *every* school day.

Changing Classroom Habits

For many years, frequent classroom observations around the country have brought me to at least one firm conclusion: As kids get older and move through the educational system, there is less intentional movement in the classroom. I have had teachers tell me that seated, quiet kids are well-behaved kids; having them move more would likely lead to chaos and a loss of control. Allen (2010) encourages teachers to think carefully about this:

> If our students are uncomfortable, fidgeting, and incapable of concentrating on our lesson, making them sit still only gives us the *illusion* of control. So, let us surrender this illusion, and deal with the reality that student engagement requires them to move—frequently. (p. 101)

Rather than fighting the students' natural inclination to move, teachers can enhance cognition by getting them up and moving. This has the happy effect of cutting down on classroom-management problems because, simply put, the level of student boredom drops.

When I coach teachers, I typically spend 30 minutes in a classroom, and I spend that time observing the students—not the teacher. If the students are seated for the entire half hour, I often notice body language (yawning, gazing at the window, tapping a pencil, passing notes, or making any number of exaggerated gestures) that indicates an increasing level of disengagement. Teachers often put this kind of behavior down to "students who no longer want to learn!" Any teacher who thinks this is a uniquely modern comment based on "the kids not being the way they used to be" might consider that when I started teaching in 1971, we sat around the faculty lounge and said the same thing. Continually playing the blame game is frustrating and draining, and it is simply not productive.

It is indeed true that kids have changed. Teenagers who stay up until the wee hours, texting and checking Facebook in their bedrooms, drag themselves to school in the morning. Sheryl Feinstein (2004), in *Secrets of the Teenage Brain,* points out that puberty brings with it a hormone (melatonin) that causes teens to go to bed later and sleep well into the next morning—assuming they have a choice. High schools that begin classes as early as 7:30 a.m. disrupt this natural pattern, and kids come to school tired and grumpy. Many districts have shifted their start time for high schools because they understand the value of a bit of extra sleep for their students.

Regardless of when the school day begins, when one high-school student after another begins to nod off in a 90-minute block, it may be easy to blame the student. In fact, much of the problem could be solved by making students less passive and more active—and that includes getting them up and moving as much as possible. I recommend that teachers in middle and high school *do something different* every 10 minutes or so. If the kids have been sitting, have them stand and engage in a paired or group activity. If they have been standing, have them sit and do something else. If they have been working *individually* for 10 minutes, let them stand and find a partner for a purposeful conversation about what they just read or wrote about. Teachers need to work movement into their plans; the alternative is to let students work movement into *their* plans. When teachers do not allow for movement, or for brief periods of exercise, classroom-management issues invariably come to the surface.

Harnessing Movement as a Tool

Over the years, I have had the pleasure of visiting scores of classrooms where teachers understand the importance of getting kids up and moving on a regular basis. In classrooms where this is *not* the case, students tend to become increasingly fidgety and disengaged. Teachers who clearly understand the relationship between exercise and cognition make certain their students don't have to sit too long without a change of pace in the form of standing, moving, and interacting with other classmates.

I can report that, in my early days of teaching, I believed that if I could get my students to simply sit there and remain quiet they would be able to concentrate and focus. It never occurred to me that a brain break every few minutes might help them focus when they sat back down. I failed to consider that *I was the only one in the room* able to move, talk, gesture, and otherwise satisfy my urge to fidget. I strolled while lecturing; I walked around the perimeter of the room while my students were watching a video; I ambled up and down the rows while they were taking a quiz or test. In short, *I moved* while *they sat* and took notes. Looking back on it, I'm surprised they did not all fall asleep or run screaming from the classroom.

One timeless ritual teachers can modify to allow for more movement in the classroom is the distribution of handouts and other materials. On more occasions than I can count, I stood at the front of each of five rows and gave the first person in each row enough worksheets, test sheets, or handouts for everyone in the row. Once again, the kids stayed seated while I walked along the front and distributed the materials. One way to change this is to have students stand up and go get the handout somewhere in the room to the accompaniment of an upbeat song ("The Wanderer?"). The music and the movement serve as energizers, and the whole task can be accomplished in the same approximate amount of time it used to take to give a handout to each student. Or, the teacher can simply fan out the sheets of paper in her hand, throwing them up in the air and letting them cascade down while students scramble for them. An appropriate song can accompany the event ("Let It Snow?"). The resultant movement and laughter at this novel way to distribute paper can once again serve as a great energizer.

Emma Jeter—Grade 5 Math/Science

While I was in her classroom, Jeter's fifth graders were taking a math quiz; she had them pause twice and stand in order to do the "chicken dance" before resuming their seats and continuing with the quiz. She did this because she understands the connection between exercise and cognition, and she put that understanding to good use during the quiz. Frequent movement is a hallmark of Jeter's lesson plans, and painted on her classroom floor is a number grid on which students practice basic mathematical computations. The kids in her classroom love being able to get up and move frequently; it should be pointed out that 100% of her students passed the state math exams the first year she transitioned from a traditional to a more-active classroom. Also notable is the fact that Jeter was one of two teachers on the fifth-grade inclusion team at her school. She clearly understands that students in special-education programs are often highly kinesthetic learners who really value the change of pace.

I can personally attest to the fact that the fifth graders in Jeter's care love coming to that classroom. She puts a great deal of time and effort into frontloading success by creating lessons and activities that require movement. I observed her classroom for the better part of three hours. The students were never seated for more than a few minutes, and she used music to get them to and from their seats. The contrast between this and traditional classrooms (lots of seat-work, videos, lecture, and worksheets) is stark. Fifth graders, who have a natural inclination to move, sing, dance, wiggle, fidget, and talk, find an outlet in Jeter's classroom. Moreover, they often go home and talk about what they did in class today—without being prompted. We interviewed one parent who said her twins talked incessantly about what happened most days; she said the evening meal often resembled dinner theater.

Marylise Cobey—Elementary Special Education

Cobey takes every opportunity to encourage movement. In her special-education classroom, she has replaced her chairs with stability balls. According to Cobey, her students love being able to bounce while they work; the use of the stability balls allows them to move and concentrate at the same time. One student who had been procrastinating on a writing assignment in another classroom was sent to her class to complete the work. Sitting on one of the stability balls at an empty desk, he went to work. A few minutes later, he looked up and said to Cobey, "I finished—how did I do that?" He had rolled, bounced, and written his way to assignment completion.

In Cobey's classroom, seatwork can be done at the students' desks or anywhere space is available. The kids are the ones who stand and get the supplies when needed; they take hokey pokey breaks during nine-weeks testing; her review games involve movement. Cobey has them do exercises frequently. Movement is also incorporated into the songs she writes for science and social studies units. Cobey's students respond well to this purposeful movement, and it has become an important part of her instruction.

Movement in the Middle

As a former middle-school social studies teacher, I have always been fond of telling people that teaching a class of seventh graders is like trying to hold 30 balloons under water simultaneously. Early in my teaching career, my students always seemed to want to sharpen a pencil, go to the restroom, head for the wastebasket to throw away a piece of paper, or otherwise fidget to the beat of a drummer other than my good self. As someone who held a very traditional view of classroom process, I tried to keep the lid on all this seemingly unnecessary motion. As the days passed during any given week, I became more and more exhausted as I wondered what other professions might pay a living wage while providing far less pain and suffering.

Not all the pain and suffering was mine. My attempts to get the kids to sit still and hunker down was, through the lens of hindsight, a little like holding the lid tightly closed on a pan of boiling pasta; the results are predictable and messy. Like many educators at the time, I had no understanding of the positive relationship between movement and learning. We have a far better understanding of this now, and, as reported by Jensen (2005), "Evidence from imaging sources, anatomical studies, and clinical data shows that moderate exercise enhances cognitive processing" (p. 67). Every day, these connections become clearer, but this was far from the case in the 1970s and 1980s.

It was not until the early 1990s that I began to design lessons to get my students to move more in the classroom, although these were admittedly tentative steps. I made this course correction because the special-education teacher on our (inclusion) team took me aside and told me that students in special education were often highly kinesthetic; those kids needed to stand and move frequently. We also had a number of ADHD students on our team, and the more I researched that topic, the more I recognized that I had a good deal in common with those kids. The difference was, of course, that I could move anytime I wanted in my classroom; it slowly began to dawn on me that movement needed to be an integral part of the lessons for students as well.

With the help of that special-education teacher, I began to shift the workload from myself to those seventh graders. I involved them more, and at one point I even had my sixth-period class write a play in class, with each of six groups of students working on a different act of a play on the impact of the Fugitive Slave Act and the Dred Scott Decision on slavery and the coming of the Civil War. My job was not to lecture, as I had been used to doing over the years, but to *facilitate process,* and I can remember how enjoyable an experience that was.

The most amazing part was that it was totally serendipitous. Writing the play, and letting them move around the room in order to dovetail action in the various acts of the play, was not in my lesson plan; I scrapped whatever I had been going to do, divided the students into groups on the spot, and let them go.

If there was one seminal moment in my transformation from a passive classroom to a more active one, that was it. In fact, I still have that play. I also wrote a play that year, called *Snow in April*, and the kids performed it for each other and for the camera. Again, I still have the video cassette, and I can recall the feeling of release that came to me during those two years as I began to get my seventh graders up and moving, interacting, creating, and otherwise far more involved in their own learning process than in previous years. I had them give speeches (optional), and one 13-year-old girl (in special education) gave a speech on abolitionism so moving that her classmates gave her a standing ovation. It was marvelous, and that year (1993–1994) marked my transition from chief lecturer and grand poobah to a facilitator of process; my students did more, and I did less, and we all enjoyed it immensely.

One problem with teaching in one's own classroom day after day is that we seldom get to observe *process* objectively. We're so busy trying to orchestrate the action from the stage that we miss the perspective that comes with being able to observe what is happening *from the balcony*. I finally had the opportunity to do that as an instructional specialist, when part of my job was to observe all social studies teachers new to our school district. From a desk in the back of the classroom, I was able to watch the teacher and the students. While my task was to observe the teacher "in action," I learned more by watching the kids. Were they interested? Were they engaged? Were they asleep? My seat in the balcony opened my eyes, and it began to open my mind.

Shortly after accepting the instructional specialist position, I was placed in charge of professional development for the office. At a national conference, I saw Laura Lipton and Bruce Wellman, coauthors of *Pathways to Understanding: Patterns and Practices in the Learning-Focused Classroom* (2000). The idea of shifting classrooms from teacher-centered to learner-centered places seemed to make perfect sense, and I brought Lipton and Wellman to our school district as soon as I could arrange it. In their workshops, we paired, we processed information in groups, and *we moved frequently.* The combination of my observations in middle-school social studies classrooms and that two-day workshop completed my transformation from running a passive to an active classroom. Teachers who provide frequent opportunities for students to stand, pair, and process information move their classrooms in the direction of a more learner-centered environment.

Below are two excerpts from language-arts lesson plans, and I include them because they highlight movement in the pursuit of collaboration.

Kathy Galford—Grade 6 Language Arts

To the accompaniment of an upbeat song, Galford's sixth graders stand and join classmates at one of six charts affixed to the walls. Each chart has one of the six figures of speech (simile, metaphor, hyperbole, etc.) labeled at the top. Each group has a different colored marker, and one student serves as recorder as students in that group create a graffiti wall—listing definitions, examples, or descriptions on the chart. Music moves them from station to station as groups get a chance to contribute to each chart in turn. The recorder changes with each transition, and the number of sentences grows as the activity continues; groups wind up at their original chart at the end, where they are given an opportunity to see what has been added during the exercise. This 10-minute activity, called a gallery walk or walkabout, involved Galford's students in something that was at once auditory, visual, and kinesthetic.

The activity described above is one among many components of a 50-minute lesson plan intended to deepen the students' understanding of figures of speech. Every component of Galford's lesson contains aspects of collaboration, and the movement in this and other activities connected to figures of speech does a beautiful job of enlisting exercise in support of cognition and memory. I watched the students for the entire time, and they were focused and engaged for every facet of the walkabout, as well as for the other activities in the lesson. She modeled or gave instructions—and they *did*. She modeled— they *did*. She facilitated process, and she listened to the groups and read the charts; this gave her some things to say when it was over. By working her way around the room, she discovered what she needed to do to clear up any misunderstandings or fill in gaps in students' learning that became apparent. Galford has found a way to move her students from seatwork to feetwork, harnessing their desire to *stand, move,* and *share*.

Moving up one grade level to seventh-grade language arts, grammar is the focus of an activity meant to review the rules of comma usage. Dani Crawford created sentences subsequently typed on index cards that were then laminated for frequent use. Each student is given a dry erase marker and one of the laminated cards prior to the start of the activity.

Dani Crawford—Grade 7 Language Arts

As the students look to the four corners of the room, they see wall posters labeled as follows:

Poster 1: Use a comma before conjunctions in a compound sentence.

Poster 2: Use commas to set off and enclose an appositive phrase.

Poster 3: Use a comma after an introductory clause phrase at the beginning of a complex sentence.

Poster 4: Use commas to show quotations in conversations.

When the music begins, students look at their laminated cards and make corrections using the markers. Fred, for example, finds he has a card with the following sentence: "Skippy's neighbor Mr. Rogers just returned from his vacation to Hawaii." Using his marker, Fred corrects it to read, "Skippy's neighbor, Mr. Rogers, just returned from his vacation to Hawaii."

Having made the correction, Fred glances around the room, and then moves to Poster 2: Use commas to set off an appositive phrase. Cindy is already there, and Fred and Cindy share how their cards demonstrate why the comma rule on Poster 2 applies to their sentences. This happens in all four corners of the room, and it is possible that students may be standing under the wrong poster, in which case students become teachers, and other students have to defend their choices or move to the correct poster.

Students make the needed correction; they self-sort, moving to a corner of the room; they compare (and possibly defend)—and all the while, Crawford moves about the room and listens. She models, and they do. She gives instructions, and they move.

Crawford reports that while this activity allows students a chance to review the use of commas it also gives them an opportunity to get up and move. The use of the laminated cards and dry erase markers provides a novel way to make corrections, and Crawford's role during the activity is to facilitate process. She moves around the classroom, and she listens to the conversations for concepts she might have to reinforce when the exercise is done. By simply circulating from poster to poster, she can check for understanding by listening to the explanations.

Common wisdom may dictate that grammar is not the most exciting subject in the eyes of students. My experience is that many *teachers* give it short shrift, ignoring it in favor of other, more-interesting language-arts topics. In the activity above, Dani Crawford has shown a willingness to harness the power of movement and music in a collaborative activity that students enjoy, and from which they gain a better understanding of these basic building blocks of language. Instead of wringing her hands and grabbing a fistful of worksheets, *Crawford has frontloaded the process with a novel approach to learning.*

Moving beyond the content for a moment, Crawford also has the opportunity to take a balcony view of group process. Are students working well together? If they are in the position of correcting other students, are they doing so gently and with empathy? When students are engaged in an activity that combines movement and collaboration, they are doing the work. If they are doing the work, teachers can stand back and observe in a way that can lead to process improvement the next time around. If things did not go well from a collaboration or time-management standpoint, teachers have the opportunity to involve students in identifying causes and looking for solutions.

Movement and Novelty in the High-School Setting

The brain thrives with exercise, as we saw earlier in this chapter, and it also craves novelty. Sousa (2001) affirms that, "the brain is constantly scanning its environment for stimuli" (p. 27). A classroom environment that does not provide sufficient external stimuli (music, movement, laughter, change-of-pace activities) and instead "contains mainly predictable or repeated stimuli" actually "lowers the brain's interest in the outside world and tempts it to turn to novel sensations" (p. 27). Teenagers who sit for any length of time without doing something different, novel, or otherwise out of the ordinary may turn inward and spend a good deal of time daydreaming; today's students may reach for their cell phones in order to do some clandestine texting. They thus control their environment to the extent they can without getting into trouble with the classroom teacher.

When I am writing a book manuscript, I have almost total control over when I write and when I stop writing. During the week, I typically go to a local fitness center to work out as early as 5:00 a.m. Following that, I have a bowl of cereal, watch some news on television, and then open a file on my computer to begin work on whatever manuscript is in the pipeline. As much as I love writing, I find my brain pulls me away in its continual search for something different or new. An e-mail will distract me, as will a visit from one of our cats. I can get up from the computer when I want to; I can get a snack in the kitchen when

I wish (too frequently, I admit); I can turn the music on or off when I desire; I can go work in our yard when I feel guilty (less frequently, perhaps); and I can simply stand and stretch when the need arises. In short, I am in total control of what I do and when I do it.

I also love listening to lectures on tape or CD while I drive. I always have one or more books on tape or lectures by prominent university professors in the car. If my mind wanders while driving, or if something the lecturer says causes me to start processing information, I may miss whole sections of the narrative or lecture. It matters not, however, because I have something magical called "stop" and "reverse" built into my car's sound system. Once again, I am in total control of my destiny (or at least of my car's stereo). I can give in to my distractions and my brain's propensity to switch gears *and still not miss anything in the lecture or book.* Once again, I call the shots.

The same cannot be said of high-school students in a 90-minute block, one of several during the day. They have no stop or pause buttons, and a high-school social studies teacher who feels the need to cover all of United States history in one school year may be moving at a breakneck pace in order to get beyond the Watergate scandal of the 1970s by spring. Information is coming so quickly to students, who may be passive (and seated) observers, that it is difficult or impossible for them to do more than take a few rudimentary notes and hope those notes and the textbook will provide some illumination in the evening or on the weekend. The truth is that the "repeated stimuli" of the high-school teacher's voice may cause many of the teenagers in the class to turn inward—and go to a better place in their minds.

The alternative is to get high-school students up and moving, sharing and processing information with each other—all to the accompaniment of music suited to the task. An upbeat song, for example, can serve as a background for moving from individual desks to pairs, trios, or small groups. The combined stimulation of the music and the movement will serve to get students ready for whatever comes next, and their brains and their bodies appreciate the change of state made possible by the teacher. A teacher who takes into account their students' need to do something different frequently is in a position to positively affect learning with various novel approaches to the content.

Julie Poclayko—Grade 11 AP Language and Composition

In Poclayko's AP class (90-minute block), she and her students study a unit on the nature and specific types of satire. Rather than facilitate a long discussion

(Continued)

(Continued)

on the topic while students sit at their desks, Poclayko sets up six different satire stations around the room. Each station is designated a "crime scene" and students rotate from station to station in 10-minute segments. At each station, song passages or video clips provide clues as to the type of satire on display. Students collaborate in groups of four: One serves as recorder, another as head of investigation, and the final two play the role of forensics specialists whose job it is to identify clues as to the type of satire it might be. At each station, the group's task is to identify the correct type of satire, so the recorder can, after writing down the observations and clues, finish the task by recording the satire type.

Poclayko's role during this extended activity is to facilitate movement from station to station, and for this purpose, she uses music. Soft music plays during station visits, and near the end of the 10 minutes, she brings the volume up and then cuts it off. The groups then rotate to a new station, switching roles in the process. By so doing, everyone gets to serve as recorder, forensics specialist, and head of investigation. Poclayko circulates around the room, keeping track of the time and listening to the conversations.

Final Thoughts

At every grade level, movement can serve to enhance memory and cognition. It also gives students a chance to stand, stretch, and travel a short distance in the classroom in order to meet with a partner or group. The use of music makes it more powerful; and in my experience, students love moving, grooving, and dancing to an upbeat song. Music and movement serve as dynamic motivators and wonderful learning tools. The most successful of the hundreds of classrooms I have visited over the years take advantage of a student's desire to get up, move, pair, share . . . and learn from each other.

Schools and school districts that are cutting back on physical education or recess are moving in the wrong direction. "Given the powerful cognitive effects of physical activity," says Medina, "this makes no sense" (2008, p. 24). When doing horizontal or vertical planning at every level, teachers and administrators would do well to explore ways to increase opportunities for exercise. The best teachers I know use movement as a regular part of their classroom routine; administrators at every level need to encourage its use in the twin interests of health and cognition.

In Chapter 2, we'll look at the value of collaboration and student-to-student conversation. As we did in this first chapter, we'll look at some specific activities used by teachers at various grade levels around the country.

2

For Whom the
(Dinner) Bell Tolls

As the afternoon gave way to early evening, kids in the neighborhood wound down the games and headed back home for dinner. Attendance was mandatory, and in my grandparents' home we ate at the kitchen table. Once every few weeks, I was invited to our neighbors' home for the evening meal, and it was served in a room appropriately and accurately called the dining room. The two brothers in that house were my best friends, and the five of us— two adults and three kids—spent the better part of an hour eating and talking. There were no television screens in sight while we ate, and conversation was the order of the day. We learned to socialize during those meals. We discussed, we explained, we listened, and we learned to speak, reason, and tackle problems and solutions in the company of adults. We practiced on a daily basis the fine art of civil discourse . . . all without distractions.

I will not claim to speak for anyone else growing up in the 1950s, and I realize my small-town upbringing may not have been typical. However, my sense is that mealtime in a large percentage of the homes of Baby Boomers like me was an opportunity for unhurried and uninterrupted conversation. On those rare occasions when we went out to dinner at a restaurant, there were few distractions to take away from the normal level of interaction as we ordered and ate our meal. Learning to socialize happened at home and in the neighborhood as a matter of course—as a matter of *discourse*.

Over the decades, the number of "let's eat in" meals has decreased as steadily and inexorably as the number of "let's eat out" meals has increased. In one local restaurant, I recently counted 47 television screens, and the restaurant provided the technological wherewithal to make viewing those screens totally interactive. I was having lunch there one day and observed a family of five enter the room and sit at a table near me. All five (mother, father, and three young boys) immediately availed themselves of some form of technology, including cell phones, video games—not to mention the 47 screens around the room. Their involvement in these electronic pursuits precluded conversation among them for the half hour they were in the restaurant. Here was the perfect opportunity for nearly 30 minutes of prime conversation; but from what I observed, the time for those five family members passed in individual pursuits. They were at the same table, but they could have been miles apart.

Once again, I don't claim that what I observed in that restaurant constitutes the norm for families today. I am sure there are families where distractions at mealtime are kept to a minimum in an attempt to get everyone involved in discussions of import. The content of those dinner-table conversations may not be as important as the opportunity they provide *for kids to practice the art of civil discourse.* In those mealtime conversations while I was growing up, we learned to allow others to talk as we listened to what they had to say. The adults at the table facilitated this informal collaboration, and we as kids felt comfortable sharing and otherwise contributing to the general discussion. There was, I believe, what Costa (2008) calls a "sense of 'us'" in those dinner-table discussions.

These conversations, of course, were informal and casual, but they were proving grounds for four essential norms that Costa (citing Baker, Costa, & Shalit, 1997) lists as *pausing* (taking turns), *paraphrasing* (seeking to understand), *probing and clarifying,* and *paying attention to self and others* (Costa, 2008, p. 117). When five members of a family can sit together in a restaurant for almost 30 minutes and pursue their own electronic interests, it is to the detriment of what Costa calls "collegial interaction" (p. 116). To the extent this is the case nationally, it has tremendous implications for teachers who are determined to create a collaborative atmosphere in the modern classroom. Teachers may increasingly have to deal with a communication deficit on the part of the students they serve. In this chapter, we'll stay with our discussion of movement in the classroom, and we'll shift our focus to student-to-student conversations. While students can certainly have paired or group conversations while seated, movement provides a change of state (not to mention increasing the flow of blood, oxygen, and glucose); it also provides a transition between whatever the students were doing while seated to a standing student-to-student discussion. With a partner, or in a group, students can explain, illustrate, describe, and summarize—all in a way that says they understand the topic under consideration. While these discussions are underway, teachers can move around the classroom from pair to pair, or group to group, as they listen to what is being said (or left unsaid). The important thing is that students are given practice at developing and mastering oral-communication skills in a deliberate and purposeful way. Students *do*, while the teacher facilitates process and tunes in to the discussions.

Old Skills and New Applications

In an age where being able to communicate clearly and effectively is becoming more important, students need to practice the art of give and take in conversation. If the old foundation for basic social discourse is being eroded, America's classrooms need to take up the slack. Trilling and Fadel (2009) point to a need for a shift in thinking for K–12 education:

> While education has always been concerned with the basics of good communicating—correct speech, fluent reading, and clear writing—digital tools and the demands of our times call for a much wider and deeper personal portfolio of communication and collaboration skills to promote learning together. (p. 54)

It is no longer enough for students to do seatwork on their own, if what is increasingly required by employers is frequent and effective collaboration in the workplace. Successful collaboration begins, at least in part, with students who practice the art of conversation and dialogue with each other, in pairs or in groups.

Tony Wagner (2008), while doing the research for his book *The Global Achievement Gap*, spoke with business owners and executives all over the country. Wagner found that poor communication skills surfaced as a concern in many of those interviews. A corporate vice president and former English teacher admitted that in his company they are "routinely surprised at the difficulty some young people have in communicating: verbal skills, written skills, presentation skills" (p. 35). He went on to say that many employees "are unable to communicate their thoughts effectively" (p. 35).

In a chapter where we will deal with oral-communication skills, we are left with one salient and perhaps unassailable point; in order for students to be able to communicate effectively, they have to practice in both lanes of the communication highway: listening and speaking. There is no shortcut here. Proficiency in anything comes as a result of practice. Students who were once able to practice their communication skills outside the classroom and at the dinner table are going to need to practice those skills *in our nation's classrooms* if they are to become proficient, confident, and contributing members of a global economy where teamwork and communication form an essential skill set.

Face to Face and Toe to Toe

When we spent whole mornings and afternoons playing outside in the 1950s, it was necessary for us to be physically present in order to play kick the can, tag, red rover come over, four square, and all the other games that were part of our outdoor repertoire. We learned the rules of the games in our own neighborhoods, and if kids with different rule variations for that game gathered on a Saturday morning, it presented a challenge. There were often disagreements arising from differing interpretations of those rules; we sometimes had to stop and work out other procedural difficulties; *but we worked them out,* usually to the satisfaction of everyone. We interacted *in person,* and we learned to get along and solve the problems that are an integral and inevitable part of social interactions when kids get together to play snow football or a pickup game of basketball. All that social interaction taught us to work through discord and solve problems on our own—face to face and toe to toe.

As we saw in Chapter 1, outdoor activities have been replaced by indoor pursuits, many of which are electronic. A kid who announces to his parents he is going to play baseball may mean he is going to his bedroom and video game console—not to the ball field. The interactive—and highly social—board games of the baby boomer generation (think *Clue* and *Monopoly*) might be considered *bored* games to today's generation of youth who can sit at a computer and do battle with an entire army of intergalactic aliens—all without interacting with another being from *this* planet. A heavy snowfall in my youth brought every kid in the neighborhood outside; one can imagine today that an adolescent might look outside at eight inches of snow and worry that the storm might mean a loss of electricity… and Internet access.

This is not to say that kids today don't crave contact with friends. A modern student can sit in her bedroom at home and have multiple electronic windows open on her computer, including instant messaging and more than one Internet site. With the cell phone within reach, she can be in touch with her friends while working on the paper that is due the next day. In looking at this phenomenon, Sprenger (2009) points out that today's "digital natives are motivated by a desire to be busy and in demand" (p. 36). In their pursuit of being connected with friends, though, "being physically present has become less important," while "responding instantly is highly prized" (p. 36). Sitting at a computer screen is essentially an individual pursuit; and interpersonal electronic connections with friends under these circumstances may well be short and superficial. In order to solve problems, make decisions, or simply function collegially as part of a team or organization—at school or in the workplace—students will need to learn and practice communication skills in America's classrooms.

Humans learn by explaining and by (truly) listening while others explain. We learn by telling stories and listening as others tell stories. We process information by discussing with others the video segment we just viewed. We enhance understanding by summarizing what someone just said or by asking for a point of clarification. Great classroom teachers talk about all of this with their students. Students need to ponder the value of speaking and listening as both relate to comprehension. Teachers need to lead those conversations, so students come to understand why they are being asked to have frequent discussions *about content* with their peers.

In this area of social discourse and purposeful conversation, teachers have their work cut out for them for the reasons we pointed out earlier in this chapter. Students today may not be having the kind of matter-of-fact social interactions at home that students of earlier generations once had. Students today may be involved to a lesser extent in the kind of collaborative play that forced Baby Boomers to learn to work through issues, solve problems, and otherwise get along. To the extent that the social skills kids once brought with them to school are no longer as well developed, teachers need to put students in pairs and groups, so they can have the kinds of social interactions necessary to success in the classroom, the workplace, and in life.

Getting Started

Over the years, I have had teachers tell me they are apprehensive about letting their students get up and move, or allowing them to discuss something in a small group. Yet, I have seen students indicate their appreciation at being able to do just that, as opposed to watching a video for 30 minutes or listening to a lecture for that amount of time. My suggestion to teachers who would like to make this change—but are anxious about doing it—is to have a frank discussion with students about how they feel when they have to sit for long periods of time. This involves taking a risk on the part of the teacher, but I believe that students will appreciate the candor, and I think they will also appreciate being asked for their opinions. Exercise is closely tied to cognition, movement helps kids get rid of the wiggles, and a change of pace is welcomed by students—just as it is by adults in a college class or workshop.

If kids don't get the opportunity to move in the interest of instruction, they will seek ways to move, tap, wiggle, giggle, and otherwise distract their peers. I often have the opportunity to ask questions of students in classroom settings. The teacher will step aside, and leave the floor open for me to have a conversation with the kids. Recently, I was in an elementary classroom, where I said, "Raise your hand if you enjoy being able to move frequently." Every hand in the room went up. When I asked why this was so, one young man said, "We like moving; I don't get into trouble as much as I used to!" Well said... and other heads nodded in agreement.

One of the negative consequences of keeping kids seated for long periods includes teachers continually trying to keep the lid tightly closed on a boiling pot; they may, in many instances, spend the entire day focusing on control and putting out one brush fire after another. I can speak here with some experience because, early in my own teaching career, I did just that. My object was to keep my junior-high-school students seated, quiet, and—paradoxically—engaged. I can report that it did not work. I went home exhausted at the end of many school days, and it was all I could do not to lose my temper on occasion; I did not always succeed. Jones (2007) tells us, *"emotions are contagious. You will get exactly what you give"* (p. 181). Had I to do those first years all over again, I would have given my middle- and high-school students more opportunities to move *at my direction* every few minutes. Movement can be part of the teacher's plan, or it can be part of the student's plan.

Before putting students of any age in trios or quartets, start with pairs. Have them turn to a partner and discuss something familiar to them—favorite vacations, music, meals, movies, books, or pastimes. One teacher of children with autism explained that while she could not get her students to share with the whole class, she finally got them to speak with a single partner. An individual student who is part of a group of four can sometimes hang back and let others take the lead or carry the load in terms of the conversation. The beauty of a pair is that there is nowhere to hide for either partner. If they are seated face to face, or standing toe to toe, the conversation is more likely to involve both students. The problem with putting two kids together and asking them to share in a discussion is that there is no *structure*. Who starts the conversation? If one person starts the conversation off, when does the other kick in? When do they stop? A lack of structure may mean that the conversations are short, stilted, or nonexistent.

Introducing Structure

A teacher who simply asks students to stand and share something with each other may be in for a shock when kids who are not used to having focused social interactions or long conversations in a formal setting are not able to function as part of a pair or group. Long hours in front of a computer or television do not prepare students for the kinds of social interactions teachers may expect of them. Even making eye contact can be a problem. For a Baby Boomer used to daily social interactions with the neighborhood kids or dinner-table discussions most nights of the week, focusing attention on someone else is not a problem, but this may not be the case for today's kids. What Sprenger (2009) calls the "digital brain" of today's student is wired differently, and standing in front of a partner while explaining or defending a point of view in a formal classroom setting can be a frightening experience. The only real way to get kids feeling comfortable with face-to-face discourse is to give them plenty of opportunities to practice the related skills of speaking and listening.

A teacher who puts students in pairs and asks one to listen while the other is speaking assumes the listener *is actually going to pay attention as the speaker explains something.* The problem here is that a student can *pretend* to listen while going to a better place in his mind. The listener can look at the speaker and smile, yet hear little and understand even less. To the teacher, it appears as if everything is going well. Unfortunately, while the student doing the talking may be doing an excellent job of describing or explaining something, the listener may be mentally disconnected with the process. Truly engaging the listener requires the assignment of a task that must be completed once the speaker is done talking.

In *The Active Classroom* (Nash, 2008), I provided the directions for paired verbal fluency (p. 33), a face-to-face conversation technique that requires the listener to summarize what the speaker says. (This set of directions is reprinted in Appendix A.) The idea behind paired verbal fluency (PVF) is to have one student talk, while another listens in preparation for reacting in one of three ways. In the first instance, when the speaker is finished talking, the listener can continue the discussion without repeating what her partner said. In the second iteration of PVF, when the speaker is done, the listener can summarize what the speaker said. Or, the listener can ask the speaker to clarify something she said. In each of these three versions of PVF, the listener, by his actions, *seeks to understand what the speaker is trying to convey.* A classroom teacher should always demonstrate the entire process with another teacher, or with a student who has been briefed ahead of time. Many students—and adults—need to have something modeled before they truly understand what is expected.

Using PVF increases the impact of paired conversations by requiring specific tasks of both students, while clearly defining what those tasks are. This structured-conversation strategy increases comprehension while successfully developing a valuable communication skill set for students. A student who can summarize what his conversation partner communicates demonstrates understanding and improves overall clarity and focus for both. PVF can be a valuable tool for teachers who want to engage students in their own learning while decreasing the amount of "teacher talk" in the classroom.

Kathy Galford—Grade 6 Language Arts

As part of a larger lesson intended to demonstrate comprehension of a short story Galford's students have already read, she asks them to stand and move across the classroom, choosing a partner in the process. Once paired, students are instructed to decide who will be Partner A and who will serve as Partner B for the PVF activity. That done, Galford designates Partner A as the one who will complete one or more of the following sentence stems related to the short story:

- *If I were in the main character's shoes . . .*
- *I thought the story was . . .*
- *I was confused by . . .*

In this first instance, then, Partner A talks while Partner B listens in preparation for her important role as summarizer. Once everyone is finished with that first conversation, Galford explains that Partner B will now have the opportunity do the talking, responding to the following question:
What is the setting of this story, and could this story take place in any other place? Why?
With the tables turned, Partner B talks and Partner A has the opportunity to summarize. In this way, both partners get a chance to explain in one role and summarize in another.

This activity, of course, is part of a much more elaborate lesson plan based on the short story in question; at every step in the process, students are fully engaged, and Kathy Galford's role is one of process facilitator. Galford understands that mastering process precedes the introduction of content. Therefore, she is careful to make certain that students get plenty of practice with eye contact, speaking, listening, and summarizing during the early PVF sessions, which help students master these critical communication skills. Once they have become used to speaking in structured-pair activities while discussing their favorite meals, books, movies, or pastimes, only then does she introduce content into the PVF mix.

Walking, Talking, and Charting

As a central-office administrator for the Virginia Beach City Public Schools, I had occasion to fill in for a high-school science teacher who was going to be absent on the last day of high school—ever—for his seniors. It was a 90-minute block, and the teacher asked me to work with them on interpersonal and collaborative skills. To accomplish this, I brought to the classroom four chart stands and some markers. I had the students count off, at which point they moved in numbered groups (to the accompaniment of upbeat music) to the charts. Each chart contained a series of questions the students had to answer, using a brainstorming process. One of the members in each group had a marker, and they charted the answers before music moved them in a clockwise fashion to the next chart and the next set of questions.

Once all four groups (6 seniors in each group) had visited each chart and recorded their input, they returned to their original charts. Then, each group picked a reporter, and those students stayed at the charts while the other members of their groups went to their seats. The reporters each relayed to all of us what was on the charts, and I asked some questions. This led to some good discussion, and we applauded each reporter in turn as they sat down. The whole activity—laced with movement, music, and conversation—lasted a little over an hour.

Next, we debriefed the process. We talked about what was necessary for groups to work together well, and I explained why I used music as part of the activity. Finally, I asked them if they enjoyed it, and the overwhelming response was yes. One student said they liked it because they were treated like adults—no worksheets, no lecture—*they* got to move, collaborate, report out, and come to some conclusions as the result of that collaboration. They were involved, engaged, and appreciative.

This strategy is called, variously, a *walkabout* or *gallery walk*; it combines movement, collaboration, explanation, reflection, conversation, analysis, synthesis, and in the above case, one or two of the students actually defended their groups' point of view to the class. In one hour, we moved up the cognitive ladder from knowledge to evaluation with a group of 24 seniors who appreciated the effort—and the chance to move—and they embraced the concept of the walkabout. Over the past 16 years, I have observed walkabouts in almost every grade level from the first through the twelfth grade. What follows is a high-school example from a social studies class whose teacher uses this powerful collaborative strategy frequently and effectively.

Deni Trombino—World History I

On many occasions in her World History I classes, Trombino has students participate in walkabouts by rotating in small groups from station to station. Each station may display art or architecture, diagrams, short excerpts from primary source materials, maps, or other course-related content. Groups work together to process the material at each station, and they record findings on a foldable graphic organizer. Once the walkabout itself is completed, students use their notes to write reviews of the material observed during stops at the various stations. In order to give the students choice, Trombino allows them to work individually or with a partner or small group to complete their written reviews. In this way, students who prefer to reflect alone get to do so, while others who would rather collaborate may do that as well.

Trombino also uses the walkabout as a check for understanding. Once again, students move in groups from chart to chart, dealing with a topic, concept, or question written on a sheet of paper. In one minute, groups dump as much information as possible on the chart in front of them, after which they are instructed to shift to the next chart and repeat the process with the new topic or question. Each group adds information, and group members are empowered to evaluate the information they see for accuracy, eliminating what they believe to be incorrect information in the process. When the activity is done, the students are able to pinpoint gaps in their learning, and Trombino knows what she needs to cover by way of review or clarification.

While it is important to give students practice at working in pairs or groups to process information, teachers should recognize that some students do enjoy working by themselves. In the example above, Trombino acknowledged this fact by allowing students to choose to work individually, or in pairs or small groups, in order to write their reviews using their own notes. Students who prefer working alone appreciate the opportunity to do so on occasion, and teachers can work into their planning occasions when they can do just that. As we observed, Trombino followed the highly interactive walkabout activity with the opportunity for some personal reflection and synthesis on the part of those members of her history class who were so inclined. Her willingness to differentiate in this way honors and supports those in her class who process information differently.

Reserve a Balcony Seat in Other Classrooms

There are many excellent reasons for teachers to visit other classrooms. Teachers who take the time to observe classes in the same building, in other schools within the district, or in schools in neighboring districts can learn a great deal—especially if they take the time to reflect on the experience soon after the observation is complete. By looking for specific things during the visit (use of wait time, opportunities for student-to-student conversations, body language and facial expressions exhibited by the teacher, etc.), teachers can answer those questions and determine to adapt and apply that which is useful in their own classrooms. Purposeful, meaningful classroom visits can accomplish much.

There is something really powerful visiting teachers can do during those classroom visits that will inform their own instruction: They can spend most of the time looking, not at the teacher, *but at the students.* Their body language, facial expressions, and actions during class can tell us a good deal about whether or not they are engaged or bored. One of the problems for a classroom teacher in her own class is that she must do a gazillion things at once; she can't simply sit back and observe the kids without worrying about materials, minor disruptions, or time. Teachers who can sit off to the side and take a sort of balcony view are better able to read the faces, reactions, and body language of all the students. I have found that looking at the kids while observing a class tells me a great deal about the efficacy of the lesson.

Administrators and lead teachers can identify classrooms where student interaction is a priority. Teachers, particularly new teachers, need to spend some time in the balcony of those classrooms, observing both students and teachers. In districts where lessons are taped for use in online professional-development programs, central-office administrators can seek out classrooms where students are standing, pairing, and sharing successfully on a regular basis. Just as students need to have PVF modeled for them; teachers need to see that interactive strategies, such as PVF and walkabouts, can be effective *without adversely affecting the behavior of students.*

Shift Gears Often

Over the years, after observing hundreds of classrooms, I can say with certainty that kids have to move. It does not much matter how old they are; they have to move. I have watched the strain on the faces of middle- and high-school teachers who lecture for extended periods of time; much of their stress comes from the fact that as the class period unwinds, an increasing number of students are eyeing the pencil sharpener, getting up to throw something in the wastebasket, tapping a pencil on a desktop, or trying to get the teacher's attention in order to ask permission to go to the restroom. In some classrooms, the restroom pass is simply handed from one student to another, much as a runner in a relay might pass the baton to a teammate running the next leg of the race.

I have seen it in college classrooms and elementary classrooms. One teacher whom I observed years ago kept the third graders in the classroom seated and working quietly for 30 minutes. I can report that as the minutes ticked by, changes began to take place: Things stored in the shelves attached to the underside of student desks competed for the attention of the kids; heads began to bob, and pencils fell off the desks; eyes began to close; the flight of birds in the yard outside the window beckoned; *and students went to greater and greater lengths to avoid the assigned task in favor of movement or social interaction.*

The beauty of having students stand when they have paired conversations or meet in groups is that they have to move to get there. Music can accompany the transition from seatwork to "feetwork," and the kids get to move on their way to doing something with a partner or group. Students can certainly stay in their seats and turn to a partner on occasion in order to have a discussion, but the movement increases the blood flow, as we have seen, and it gets them mentally ready to have the conversations. They change their physical state and their mental state, the latter through a shift from individual seatwork to collaborating with another student. Being on their feet offers a change, and working with a partner accomplishes that as well.

Talking It Over With Students

There is no reason why teachers and students should not have a candid conversation about the benefits of purposeful movement and student-to-student conversation in the classroom. There is no grade level from K to 12 where this conversation cannot be productive. High-school teachers, for example, can explain that students will frequently stand and collect handouts, move to another part of the room to meet with a partner, shift to another desk or table to meet with someone other than those next to whom they ordinarily sit, walk around the room with a group as they write on wall charts in a walkabout, take part in an activity where they stand rather than sit, and stand (as an option) when they begin their homework. Moving three or four times in the course of a 90-minute block is something students may well appreciate. Add upbeat music to the mix, and teachers are on to a winner.

Final Thoughts

Combining movement with opportunities for student-to-student discourse on a frequent basis addresses the brain's need for novelty. Students who get practice in explaining, describing, summarizing, analyzing, and coming to conclusions are building life and work skills that will serve them well down the road. At the same time, the brain gets an increased blood flow (carrying oxygen and glucose, for energy) when students stand and move, and the students' communication skills get a workout when teachers provide opportunities for structured conversations.

In Chapter 3, we'll focus on what teachers can do during the summer and through the first five days of school to increase the likelihood that students will be engaged and successful.

3

Setting the
Table for Success

I once observed a sixth-grade classroom where the kids were up and moving no fewer than three times during the class period, and it was music that got them where they were going. They stood, moved, shared, and sat down; and they thanked each other for sharing without being prompted. When they were seated, they worked smoothly in quartets, using sort cards provided by the teacher. Seated or standing—they did the work while the teacher facilitated process. In no time at all, I understood clearly that the kids had done this many times before; they had the procedures down pat. The time flew by for all of us, and at the end of the period the teacher dealt with a couple of content pieces she had noticed needed attention when she was circulating around the classroom observing her sixth graders in action. It was one of the best lessons I have ever seen, and the kids not only did most of the work but they also demonstrated a mastery of procedures (moving, meeting, discussing, acknowledging, and responding quickly to visual and auditory cues). The seeds for what I observed were planted and nurtured during the first five days of school by a teacher who put the process horse in front of the content cart.

In the first two chapters, we returned to two favorite themes from my first book, *The Active Classroom* (Nash, 2008), and we checked in with several teachers who incorporate these two themes—movement and processing information through student-to-student conversations—into their lesson plans as a matter of course. The key to success for classrooms as engaged and effective as these is what happens in the first week of school. Every teacher on the planet wants his or her classroom to run smoothly. Every teacher understands time is of the essence; this being the case, it is essential that time not be wasted. The most successful classrooms I have visited are those in which events unfold smoothly and purposefully. During those observations, it becomes quickly apparent whether or not teachers have spent enough time frontloading success by emphasizing *process* during the first week with students.

In *The Active Teacher* (Nash, 2009), I stressed the importance of using those first five days with students to turn classroom procedures into routines. Wong and Wong (2005) provide a three-step approach to success—an investment that will pay dividends for the rest of the school year. Teachers must first explain, model, and demonstrate the procedure to the students. The second phase involves rehearsing the procedure under the supervision of the teacher. In the final analysis, the practiced procedure becomes routine (p. 174).

For example, many elementary teachers use music to line their kids up when it is time to leave the classroom. The only time those teachers play that particular piece of music is when it is time to line up. One teacher uses the Johnny Nash song "I Can See Clearly Now" to get students to clean off their desks and line up quietly along the wall in front of the classroom door. In this case, the teacher does not have to say anything at all; she simply plays the song. Often, as soon as the kids hear it, they start singing along; and while singing they clean up, push their chairs under the tables, and then move toward the door, lining up in the order they reach the wall. It is smooth, fun, and effective. The teacher has them do this over and over again during the first few days of class; she fine tunes it and works out the kinks—and one more procedure is part of her class-room structure. They simply do it, and they sing their way out the door. On more than one occasion, when music cues a behavior, I have found myself singing as well.

There are many transitional events that can make or break a class-room. Here are a few:

- Students entering the room
- Elementary students moving from desks to a rug
- Students changing from one set of materials to another for a new activity or lab
- Students standing and pushing their chairs under the desks in preparation for a transition of some sort

- Students moving to work in standing pairs or groups and back again
- Students thanking each other after sharing, before moving elsewhere
- Students turning to a seated partner to have a conversation
- Teachers handing out materials
- Students handing in completed assignments
- Teachers collecting homework
- Students lining up to leave the classroom

Consider the first item on the list: students entering the room. In secondary schools, this between-bell transitioning happens several times per day. I have observed classrooms where students enter the room, quickly and quietly take care of their belongings, and begin work on a bell ringer—all this while the teacher stands at the door and greets students. I have seen other classrooms where students wander around the room, continue to talk with friends after the door closes, and fail to go to their own seats—even after the teacher requests they do so. It is not difficult to determine in these two examples which teacher spent the first several days of school on procedures, and which teacher handed out the books on the first day, rushed into the content, and trusted that everything else would fall into place. A teacher who wants students to enter the room in a certain way and get to work in a certain amount of time *must practice that over and over again until the procedures become routine.*

The teacher who takes care of the most basic of procedures *up front* will be able to insert more-elaborate processes later on. If students learn *on the first day of school* how to enter the room in an orderly fashion, arrange their work space, push their chairs under the desks, and give the teacher their undivided attention—all on cue—teachers will be in a much better position to take the next step in student engagement: transitioning to meet with a partner, trio, or larger group somewhere in the classroom for the purpose of processing information through conversation. A teacher who has not taken the time to master the most basic procedures *will not take that next step.* I have had teachers look around their own classroom room, laugh, and ask me if I can imagine "these students" meeting and discussing anything. Yet "these students" will go down the hall, enter *another* classroom, *and do just that.* Getting students to do what is necessary has nothing to do with magic or the luck of the draw; it has everything to do with planning the work and working the plan.

This emphasis on putting in place a smooth-running set of procedures is evident in Stephanie Meister's first-grade classroom.

Stephanie Meister—Grade 1 Teacher

During the first week of school, Meister relentlessly works on procedures; her first graders practice transitioning, cleaning up, and lining up over and over again until these activities become routine. In this effort, she enlists the help of music as a process facilitator. The song that serves as a cue for cleaning up and transitioning to another activity is Beyond the Sea *(Kevin Spacey version). Meister does not tell her students to clean up and prepare to do something else; she simply hits the play button on her remote. Observing one morning in Meister's classroom, I watched as the kids began to clean up and get ready for the next lesson segment or activity. They "grooved" as they straightened up their desks.*

One morning, a guest reader in Meister's class waited to begin reading her story, and marveled as the kids shifted from one place to another in a short period of time, all without delay or complaint. The music did the work. Their desks straightened, another song moved the first graders from their desks to their places on the rug, and the only talking Meister did was to introduce the reader to the students. This seamless transition was accomplished using two songs, and the kids loved it.

Meister regularly involves her students in discussions about what the class should look like and sound like during regular activities. Their ideas are charted and posted on the wall, and these charts are reviewed before and revisited after the activities. These lists of expectations—created by the students—give them ownership of process, and these regular reminders and discussions help make things run smoothly in her classroom.

Meister also has her first graders practice how to turn and talk to each other (knee to knee and toe to toe). She models this with her students, and she also models how they should thank partners after sharing. A few short weeks into the school year, her students thank each other without being asked.

One way of getting students to clean off their desks, as we saw in the example above, is to play a piece of music that sends the signal that it is time to clean up. Visuals can also be used to let students see exactly what materials are needed for the next activity. For example, some teachers use digital cameras to take pictures of what they want the student desks to look like. If, for example, they want the kids to get out their math books, a blank sheet of paper, and a pencil, they simply display on the screen a *picture* of a desk with a math book, a blank sheet of paper, and a pencil (Figure 3.1). In this case, auditory

Figure 3.1   Visual Instructions Are Clear and Unambiguous

Photo by Dana Hand. Used with permission.

instructions (which may be missed or misunderstood by students) are replaced by a *simple visual* (not open to misinterpretation). After that first week, the teacher no longer has to tell the kids how to arrange their desks or what materials to gather; the picture does that for her. It is a cheap and effective method, and teachers who use it no longer have to listen to students say, "What did you tell us to do?"

A high-school science teacher has found that by taking pictures of her lab tables with whatever is needed for that day's lab, students no longer get the wrong size beakers or test tubes. Science teachers have cupboards full of materials, and using the visual beats using the auditory when it comes to setup—and it saves time. Additionally, in a classroom where safety is of primary concern, a clear and unambiguous picture of what needs to be done by students before the lab begins is worth a great deal.

Another procedure that is critical to classroom management is the norm established by the teacher to get the attention of the students. In one elementary school, teachers at all grade levels use an identical handclapping signal to accomplish this. Every student in the building knows that signal, and the beauty of it is they have to participate by clapping with the teacher. It is visual, auditory, and kinesthetic—and in that school, it is effective. Substitute teachers who are in the building frequently learn quickly how to get the attention of the kids, no matter whose classroom they are in for the day.

The procedures for getting the attention of students, handing in homework, opening class, moving in the classroom, pairing with another student, working in trios or quartets, cleaning up, setting up, or dismissing students—all are examples of procedures that need to be mastered during the first five days of the school year. Ambiguity and confusion serve as twin enemies of a well-run classroom; getting processes firmly established during the first week of school is an excellent way to create an effective and unambiguous process flow.

Classroom Climate

Students need to feel safe in the classroom; that is, they should understand that it is safe to discuss something in a pair, in a group, or in front of the entire class without being embarrassed in some way. Students—and teachers, on occasion—can be sarcastic. Sarcasm can result in students being unwilling to share with peers or talk at all in the classroom. One of the basic tenets of the active classroom is that verbal processing on the part of students enhances memory and understanding on any given topic. However, if students refuse to share because they believe they will be brought up short by their classmates, they will not have the interactions that they need to have. During the first week of the school year, regardless of grade level, teachers need to lead students in a frank discussion of the negative effect of judging another student's opinion or introducing sarcasm into the mix. Teachers who do not deal with this in September may find that by October the classroom climate has deteriorated to the point where students are afraid to share or contribute.

I used to think I could keep my students from bringing their problems or personal feelings into the classroom. In spite of my best efforts to do this, it did not work. Unfortunately, I did not have a plan for dealing with those feelings and problems that were part of my students' lives; because of that, I never had a Plan B. I never brought into the open a candid discussion of this very human reality; frankly, I did not want to deal with it, so I told them to leave their problems at the door when they entered the room. One problem with this, of course, is that *I did not always leave my own problems or feelings at the door when I came into my own classroom.* I was telling them one thing while modeling something else. Problems and feelings are human, and it is inevitable that students will bring them into our classrooms.

Bluestein (2008) reminds us that we have to find a way to deal with this. After recognizing "that students can't simply leave their feelings at the door," Bluestein suggests teachers provide students with "a variety of healthy outlets for students to use to get their feelings out (or be heard) without creating problems for themselves or others" (p. 282). Students—and teachers—have feelings and problems that accompany them to school; the danger is that those feelings can interfere with the safe operation of the classroom. A teacher who loses his temper or turns sarcastic when challenged by a student has opened the door to such behavior on the part of his students.

One teacher has a discussion with her students during the first week of school about the need for a safe and inviting classroom environment. When any student in her class becomes sarcastic or gets out of line, others are empowered to place their fists together with their thumbs in the air and say, "Always up!" This is a visual and auditory reminder to the offender that in this classroom, negativity is not permitted. I was present one day when three students at a table used this gesture to let the fourth student know his behavior was simply unacceptable. Once again, an early investment pays off during the school year, and letting students take care of these minor infractions obviates the need for the teacher to "play cop" at every turn.

Instruction-Based Planning

As teachers approach a new school year, some instructionally based decisions need to be made, decisions that will ramp up student learning. Two key areas I suggest teachers explore include the benefits of encouraging curiosity, along with the role and nature of questioning, including ways in which teachers respond to students' answers.

Curiosity Needs to be Fed, not Bypassed

In a social studies class, a teacher projects a picture of a ship on the screen. Her students take a look at the image while she walks from the back of the room to the front. The students stare at the ship, working out for themselves what it is. There is some context available; they have been studying Ancient

(Continued)

(Continued)

Greece, and for some of them the light goes on as their brains start to make connections on the way up the cognitive ladder to inference. The mental wheels grind to a halt as the teacher, having reached the front of the room, turns to face her students. She begins to explain that this is an Athenian trireme, so called because of the three rows of oars. Each of these oars, she says, is rowed by a single person, someone who may or may not be a slave. She points out the bow that can be used as a ram, along with the rudder that steers the ship. Her description proceeds until every vestige of curiosity has been extinguished; the students who earlier were beginning to wonder about this image and its uses no longer show much interest. The fact is that their natural curiosity has been preempted by the teacher. The tacit question, What am I? that was in the air when the picture was first projected onto the screen has been answered, but not by the students.

In the National Gallery of Art in Washington, D.C., there is a beautiful watercolor by the American artist Winslow Homer called *Breezing Up (A Fair Wind)*. When I visit the museum, I invariably spend a good deal of time on a bench in front of this painting. It is a watercolor that depicts three boys and the skipper on a sailboat off the New England coast in the 1870s. I wonder about where Homer was when he painted it, and I speculate about how long it took him to finish it. Having never sailed in a boat of that size, I wonder what it must be like to take the tiller and change direction and speed—all on a lazy afternoon in the company of family and friends. At that moment, and on that bench, I don't want a curator to explain anything to me, or reveal any mysteries. The explanations and mysteries can wait, and I'll get to my own questions in time; in the several minutes I always spend in front of this, my favorite among Homer's works, I want to get lost *in my own thoughts* and speculate on my own terms. This is the promise and the magic of curiosity. I would rather draw my own conclusions and test them later against what the experts have to say.

Jensen (2005) says that curiosity, along with its sibling, anticipation, "are known as 'appetitive' states because they stimulate the mental appetite" (p. 77). Great teachers understand that the brain gets a workout when presented with a puzzle—in the instance above, a picture of a ship. The stimulation that came from wondering about what they saw was short circuited by the teacher's intervention. She told them what they were seeing. She explained what they were looking at on the screen; anticipation and curiosity *were casualties of this display of what the teacher knew.* It is not about what the teacher knows; it is about what a student sees in her mind's eye. It is about anticipation and discovery; it is about harnessing the power of curiosity.

One high-school teacher who understands the curiosity and anticipation factor created a simple but effective visual that allowed his students to wonder, question, and anticipate what he was doing.

Art Truesdell—AP U.S. History Teacher

During a class period devoted to a discussion of the War of 1812, Truesdell realized he was about to talk about the fact that the United States Government had instituted a search for more and better rifles in the decade after the war. As Truesdell talked, he went to his desk drawer and pulled out four pens. Still talking, he began to disassemble the pens, shifting parts from one pen to another. He did not explain what he was doing, and his actions were met with puzzled looks until—one by one—his juniors began to make connections between his explanation of the postwar search for more rifles and interchangeable parts. This fascinating visual image raised their curiosity levels as they tried to come to a conclusion about what he was doing, based on the contextual information they already had in their possession, along with what he was continuing to say even as he took the pens apart and put them back together. He had everyone's undivided attention, even as they attempted to make sense of it all.

In both cases, the ship projected on the screen and the interchangeable parts of the pen, it was not necessary to rush the explanation. Most of the value lay in letting students get a mental workout as they tried to put the puzzle pieces together while they built understanding and knowledge. The context of the content in both cases provided clues; and students were able to rev their mental engines a bit before all was revealed in the case of the interchangeable pen parts, whereas with the picture of the ship, that important mental exercise *was simply bypassed in order to give the students information.* Gunter, Estes, and Schwab (1999) argue that, "If knowing how to learn is more important than knowing all the answers, then the greatest realization of a person's intellectual life must be that good questions are more important than right answers" (p. 122). In the case of the ship's image, the teacher was concerned less with ramping up thinking skills than with the acquisition of information for its own sake. The information can safely follow the thought process, as Art Truesdell proved with his visual entryway into a lesson on interchangeable parts and their importance to the development of manufacturing in the United States.

Emphasize Questions, Not Answers

Life is not a multiple-choice test. Adults do not get up in the morning, pick up the paper, and try to make the correct choice for the day among four possible answers. Life is complicated; and succeeding ultimately requires an ability to think critically about a whole range of options. Humans who can use their mental faculties to sort through some pretty complicated choices are ahead of the game. The answers to tough questions may not be in front of them, neatly stacked from A through D. *Can we afford to get married at this time? Can we swing the purchase of this car? Do I rent? Do I buy? Can I sustain payments on this house? What is the impact of making only the minimum payments on one or several credit cards? Should I change jobs?* The list of life questions goes on and on, and students leaving the relatively safe and supportive school environment need to have the tools to deal with life and whatever it brings.

It is critical that teachers provide students with plenty of questions that help them develop thinking skills. Questioning sequences in a classroom may come with the rapidity of a machine gun. Teachers may ask question after question, all in a search for the "single correct answer." One of the problems with this is that, in a classroom of 30 sophomores, there may be a handful of them who feel comfortable responding to the questions. Everyone in the class realizes that the teacher knows the correct answer; the object is to find a student who can reveal it. So, the teacher asks, "Who knows the answer to this question?" Eddie, in the back of the classroom, does not know who "who" is, but he knows it isn't him. He is off the hook for the entire series of questions because there are a few members of the teacher's fan club who will take care of this. He can go to a better place in his mind. He has permission to disconnect.

Rather than ask a series of related questions intended to solicit single—and "correct"—responses, I suggest teachers ask a much more open question dealing with the topic at hand. For example, let's suppose a science teacher has just finished showing a seven-minute video on photosynthesis. The day before, near the end of the class period, she had spent a few minutes encouraging students to read some information in their text on the subject, and had encouraged them to find out what they could about photosynthesis online. Once the video is done, she does the following.

1. Standing on a small stool in the front of the room, she says, "Stand up!" (She accompanies this auditory command by bringing her hands—palms up—from her sides up into the air in a sweeping gesture.)

2. Once they are all standing, she says, "In a moment, when I say go, find someone who is not currently in front of you, behind you, or to your left or right. Stand with that person somewhere in the classroom. Ready, Go!" (She plays some upbeat music as they move.)

3. As soon as everyone is paired up, she says, "Decide who will be A and who will be B!" Next, she says, "B stands for begin. In a minute or so, I am going to ask B to explain to A all he or she knows about photosynthesis. I'll give you about 60 seconds; then, I'll stop you and ask A to summarize what B just said, adding anything he or she knows about the topic. B explains, and A summarizes—on my cue. Are there questions about process?"

4. As there are no questions, she says, "The topic is photosynthesis. Ready, Go!"

5. While B does some explaining for that first minute, the teacher walks around and listens. After the chatter begins to die down, she says, "Finish your thought and stop. A, please summarize what B told you, and add anything you want to add about photosynthesis."

6. Once again, the teacher walks around, stopping on two occasions to ask students if they would mind sharing what they just said with the entire class. Those students agree to share, and she brings everything to a halt by saying, "Finish your thought . . . pause . . . look this way."

7. When everyone is looking at her, she says, "Thank your partner for sharing, and take your seats." (She hits her remote, and upbeat music accompanies her students to their seats.)

8. Once they are seated, the teacher calls on the two students from whom she solicited their permission to share. She knows, basically, what they will say, and their comments lead into a general discussion on photosynthesis. When she does pose a couple of questions, she gives sufficient wait time (three to five seconds) before calling on anyone. This gives students a chance to think about what they might say if called upon.

What this science teacher has done is to *prime* her students for an eventual class discussion. She began by providing them opportunities to learn a bit about photosynthesis through the use of a minilecture the day before, a challenge to surf the Web for information during the previous evening, and capped it off with a short, animated video. Rather than asking single questions of the usual suspects in her class, she had her students stand, pair up, and share what they had learned. At any one time during the pair share, half the students were talking, while half were listening carefully—aware they had to summarize and add something at the end. Meanwhile, the science teacher circulated and found two students willing to share, so that later on their comments would serve as the starting point for a class discussion. She primed them for that discussion, and she allowed them to stand and move in the process; this movement, as we saw in Chapter 1, cascaded neurotransmitters and sent more blood (oxygen and glucose) to their brains.

During this 10-minute activity, the science teacher shifted students from the knowledge level to the comprehension level of the cognitive ladder. As the activity unfolded, students had a chance to explain, describe, and summarize; the teacher had an opportunity to listen to a dozen conversations as she gauged what they did or did not understand about photosynthesis. She was able to let two students share something with classmates; these were students who did not ordinarily share, and that was an accomplishment in itself. Once they were seated, she was also able to clear up some misunderstandings that she heard when circulating around the room. She used the paired verbal fluency activity (like the one we saw in Chapter 2) to prime the group for a class discussion later on. In doing so, she moved students up the cognitive ladder at least one step.

There is a critical moment after a student answers a question where the teacher's response—verbal and nonverbal—can either encourage or short circuit further involvement on the part of students. One of the best workshop facilitators I know will ask questions and then stand facing that person with his hands at his sides and a completely neutral expression on his face. The participant's answer does not change his posture or facial expression. In the questions he asks, he is not really interested in a "right" answer or even a single answer. Many answers are possible; this master workshop facilitator is not judgmental, and if he is not clear about what one of his workshop participants said, he will ask for clarification. Being in his workshops and seminars is never frightening, and participants respond freely and frequently, without fear of being "wrong."

Costa (2008) affirms, "nonjudgmental acceptance provides conditions in which students are encouraged to examine and compare their own data, values, ideas, criteria, and feelings with those of others as well as with those of the teacher" (p. 212). As teachers plan for the school year, they need to commit to creating the kind of atmosphere that encourages student participation across the board. Being nonjudgmental is a great start. Also, Costa suggests that paraphrasing is a great way for teachers to honor students by showing they understand. "While the teacher may use different words than the student, the teacher strives to maintain the intent and accurate meaning of the student's idea" (p. 213). It is important for students to understand, and they also want to be understood.

I am not saying that correct answers are not important; I am suggesting that the thought process involved in *getting* to any answer is critical. If correct answers seem to be, to students, the most important outcome, this can lead to shortcuts (cheating) to obtain those answers. Being able to explain, illustrate, describe, analyze, synthesize, infer, and defend points of view are all important in K–12 education, college, the workplace, and life in general. Questions are important. Giving students time to think about possible answers is *also* important. Responding to the answers in a way that does not betray judgment is critical to creating the kind of classroom climate in which students are willing to take risks. I have been in classrooms where students are afraid to share, either because the teacher or fellow students will judge the response. I have also visited classrooms where students are perfectly comfortable sharing with a partner, a small group, or the whole class. It is in the planning stages that teachers, working individually or in groups, can make certain through their actions that a free flow of information and conversation is maintained over the course of the school year.

Final Thoughts

Teachers and administrators need to put a great deal of thought into what they will do during the first week of school with students. Processes are critical to success, and what is done during those first 5 days will be reflected in the following 175 days. Creating a classroom climate where students can feel free to share, where teachers understand the role of curiosity and anticipation, and where students can move up and down the cognitive ladder with regularity, is well worth the effort and planning involved.

In Chapter 4, we'll look at what many years of classroom observations have led me to believe about what students want in their classrooms and in their teachers.

4

First One at
the Bus Stop

What hit me first was the realization that I was in a special classroom. I was there to observe, and my first observation was that the students in this classroom loved being there. On entering the classroom that day, I joined a group of three students who welcomed me and showed me to the fourth desk in a group of four, after which they turned to receive directions for an activity that would have them up and moving for several minutes. All the furniture in the room had tennis balls covering the leg bottoms, so the furniture could be moved easily without damaging the surface of the tile floor. There was a large, open area in the center of the room; and when the students stood, they moved the desks and chairs even farther away from the center, so there would be plenty of room for them to meet and interact in pairs and groups.

Music accompanied this moving of furniture, and the kids danced their way to the center of the newly enlarged room and paired up ... and I thought to myself, they've done this before! It took no time at all for me to understand that the students were totally engaged with a teacher who long ago realized that kids have to move, and kids have to share. One student in that classroom said that the year before she made up excuses to miss the school bus ... This year, she was the first one at the bus stop. I could see why; I knew I was in a very special place, with a very special teacher.

This elementary student went on to say that the year before had been filled with worksheets and seatwork, something that differed dramatically from her current classroom situation. I was there for hours, and I returned on many occasions to see what can be done when movement, music, student discourse, and collaboration are infused into the classroom climate on a daily basis. The students were totally engaged, and it was clear that their teacher had spent a good deal of time during the first week of school ensuring her classroom was a safe, challenging, and fun place. The parents of those students were fully supportive; and at the end of the year, there were many tears from teacher, students, and parents alike.

We often get caught up in the crunching of numbers related to standardized testing. We put in place this program or that program, and in our planning we (correctly) concentrate on what we can do to educate students. We as educators facilitate the creation of extensive strategic plans, and then we replace those with other strategic plans down the road when a newly constituted leadership team takes over. Every bit of this is fine, *if it results in positive changes in the classroom*. It is all wonderful if administrators and teachers dedicate themselves to continuous improvement. The most effective things that happen related to learning happen in the classroom. A school can have a fantastic, beautifully written, and well-intentioned strategic plan; if teachers continue to lecture, show video after video, and make individual seatwork the order of the day—substantial progress will continue to be absent from the results. When kids *want* to come to school, when kids *want* to come to class, and when kids *recognize* the benefits of their involvement—good things happen.

Observations

When visiting classrooms, I watch the students. Body language and facial expressions tell me a good deal. Students who are seated for long periods begin to show signs of disengagement: slumping postures, nodding heads, or tapping on knees or desks. How students act and what they say, often *sotto voce*, can be an indicator of whether or not they enjoy being in that classroom. The length of time it takes for students to respond to the teacher's verbal directions can speak volumes about how effective processes are in the classroom. A lack of clarity and focus on the part of the teacher can lead to ambiguity and wasted time. What follows are a few things I have noticed over the years, along with some inferences based on those classroom observations.

Students Appreciate and Support Structure

Most students don't like chaos in the classroom. Teachers who take the time to explain and practice procedures during the first week of school are putting in place a structure that will serve students well over the course of the remaining 35 weeks of school. On the other hand, teachers who are not proactive in their approach to establishing and maintaining effective procedures must continually "react to the disaster that has been created by a lack of structure" (Jones, 2007, p. 137). Some people are born organizers; they may intuitively understand the benefits of a *classroom structure* that allows for safe social interaction, efficient instructional activities, the timely completion of tasks—not to mention the classroom teacher's own sanity. The well-adjusted and confident teachers I see have one thing in common: they take the time to establish effective processes beginning on day one.

In the absence of a clear and effective set of procedures, students are often puzzled and unclear about what to do next. I have seen both sets of circumstances, and I have formed the conclusion that students prefer a clear, understandable definition of what happens when. When processes are not firmly established, the best lesson plan in the world will likely run quickly aground. My experience is that kids don't like this; they would rather have things run smoothly during a lesson or activity. Let's look at an example of what can go wrong when the basic classroom structure does not support the best-laid plans of a middle-school teacher.

> *Mrs. McGarvey attended a seminar where she heard other teachers talk about having students stand, pair, and share in class. This all sounded good to her, so she worked into her lesson plan an opportunity for her students to stand, pair up, and discuss content-specific information on the following Monday. In her first-period science class, she told the students they would be standing up soon in order to discuss something with a partner. She then explained what they would discuss. What followed caused her to question her decision to inject the activity into her lesson.*
>
> *As soon as she told her students they would be pairing up, they began to look around the room and make eye contact with likely partners; some even began asking their friends to pair with them. Her explanation of what they were supposed to discuss was lost in the ensuing chaos, as more and more students verbalized their thoughts. Some tried to shush the students who were talking and distracting others, and that led to yet more disruptions. When the students finally paired up, Mrs. McGarvey noticed that some had not even stood; half the class was standing, and half the class was seated. Some of the students started their discussions, but those—and there were many—who had not heard what it was they were supposed to discuss raised their hands in order to ask Mrs. McGarvey what it was they were supposed to be doing. By the time she sorted it all out, Mrs. McGarvey made a mental note to remove this activity from her plans for the rest of the day's classes. It had been a disaster, and she also vowed never to try it again.*

By way of a postmortem, let's take this apart to see why her attempt at paired collaboration failed. First, our fictional teacher, Mrs. McGarvey, had neglected to establish and practice a procedure to be used in paired activities. Had this been done during the first week of school, with students standing frequently in order to have paired discussions on topics of personal interest, this activity would have succeeded in its purpose of having students discuss—and by so doing increase their understanding of—a content-rich subject. What she might have done on that Monday is to have them turn to a neighbor and discuss something of interest to them (favorite vacation destinations, music, movies, books, etc.) so that they could begin to be comfortable with having the conversations. That could have been followed by having them stand and discuss something else with which they were totally familiar. These short discussions, seated and standing, might have helped pave the way for the content-related conversations at another time.

Second, when she announced they would be meeting with partners, most of them immediately began to work out in their own minds with whom they would pair. In a way that would give them a good deal of choice about partners, she could have let them use the Appointment Clock in Figure 4.1, so each student in the room

Figure 4.1   The Appointment Clock

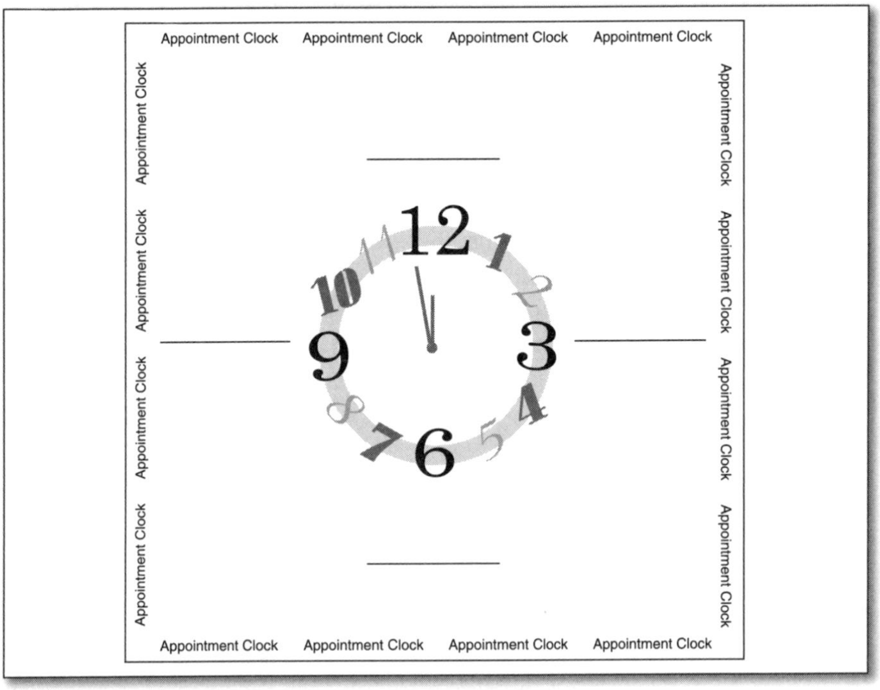

Design by Dianne Kinnison

would have a 12:00, 3:00, 6:00, and 9:00 partner with whom they could meet later on. This gives students choice up front and eliminates any confusion and time wasting when it is time to meet and discuss something down the road.

Students Want Clear Instructions

Another problem faced by Mrs. McGarvey was that she gave too many directions at one time. While her students worked out with whom they would meet, they missed the second part of her instructions that dealt with the topic of the discussion. I have observed students on many occasions when teachers give them too many directions up front, something that results in confusion and lost time when it comes time to move forward with the lesson or activity. Allen (2010) states the problem from the perspective of the student:

> Students who aren't clear about what is required may hesitate to involve themselves for fear of doing something wrong. They may quickly wander off task, or worse yet, they may believe they are on task, but end up spending precious classroom time on an inconsequential tangent. (p. 43)

The answer to this is both simple and difficult for teachers—give directions one at a time.

Let's suppose for the moment that our fictional teacher, Mrs. McGarvey, had put in place a structure that facilitated purposeful paired or group conversations among her students early in the year. That done, the students take a few minutes to establish Appointment-Clock partners (Figure 4.1). Once partners are established, the directions for the lesson we saw above might look like this:

1. Holding up an Appointment-Clock sheet, Mrs. McGarvey says, "Hold up your Appointment-Clock sheets."

2. Once all the sheets are in the air, she says, "Locate your 12:00 partner in the room, and wave at that person from your seat."

3. Having made certain that each student has a partner (one trio will exist for this discussion because Mary's 12:00 partner is absent), Mrs. McGarvey says, "Stand up! (pause) Find your 12:00 partner, and stand with that person someplace in the room." (Some upbeat, transition music here would be helpful.)

4. Standing on a short stool so that she can see everyone from above, she says, "Your discussion topic is on the screen." At this point,

she shifts in order to point to the screen with her hand, revealing with a remote the question they will answer or topic they will discuss. This gives them a visual as well as an auditory cue.

5. She then says, "When I say go, work with your partner to answer the question;" or, "When I say go, discuss with your partner as much as you know about the topic."

6. As they begin their conversations, Mrs. McGarvey steps down from the stool and begins to circulate, listening to the discussions. She hears something she wants brought up later, and she asks that student if he will share later on. She does that once more with one of the girls in the class; then, she says, "OK, 30 more seconds, please!"

7. Stepping back onto the stool, she raises her hand and says, "Pause, and look this way, please!" followed by, "Thank your partner for sharing . . . take your seats, please!" (A little transition music, please.)

8. Once they are seated, Mrs. McGarvey asks the two students who agreed to share to do that, and that leads into a guided discussion on the topic.

The bottom line here is that in classrooms where directions are given one at a time—and with great clarity—the whole lesson or activity goes much more smoothly. In cases where the instructions are bunched up at the beginning of class, students are much less likely to know what they need to do next. In these instances, student body language and facial expressions indicate to me, the observer, that they do not like confusion or ambiguity when they are asked to do something; they need to be clear about what that something is. The time saved by giving directions individually, rather than all at once, adds up over the course of a school year. More importantly, students will appreciate the efficiency and lack of ambiguity.

Students Don't Want the Sideline View

When I close my eyes and envision classrooms I have observed over the years, I am reminded of the loneliness of kids on a sports team who sit on the bench and rarely get to participate. When they go home at the end of the day, students are involved in whatever is going on there. They put *themselves* in play, and they are active participants in whatever it is they decide to do after school and on weekends. When they come to school on Monday, they are too often relegated to the role of passive observer, and whatever luster this may have fades quickly if life in school is just one lecture, video, or worksheet after another. In truly active classrooms, students are involved from the moment they enter the room, and their body language and deportment tells me—the observer in all this—that they appreciate getting into the game.

This may be the most consistent and most often reiterated theme of this entire *Active Classroom Series*. During my classroom visits around the country, I often ask students in classrooms where movement is part of the regular classroom structure, "Do you enjoy being able to move?" or, "Do you like it when you are *doing* something, rather than *watching* something?" The answer is always a resounding yes. Sometimes, they get to me first with a comment. After observing a middle-school classroom, two students thanked me, as they went out the door after class, for providing their teacher with the active-classroom strategies. They told me they loved the movement and the music; most importantly—and I want to stress this—*they love going to that classroom.* Once there, they thoroughly enjoy taking part in lessons that have them engaged and involved in their own learning.

One fourth-grade teacher who understands fully the relationship between movement and cognition also understands that her students feel the need to be actively involved and engaged. Early in the school year, Becky Bowerman discussed with her students the importance of physical activity as it relates to memory and an increased blood flow that carries with it oxygen and glucose (an energy boost). During the course of the year, Bowerman utilizes movement frequently, as she does in the following example that relates to math—and specifically, to computational fluency.

Becky Bowerman—Grade 4 Teacher

As she works with her fourth graders on their multiplication tables (up to 12 × 12), Bowerman first has students analyze trends that appear in the products of a math family. (For example, 8 × 1 = 8; 8 × 2 = 16; 8 × 3 = 24; 8 × 4 = 32; 8 × 5 = 40; etc.) Having thus identified a logical progression of products for the eights, Bowerman then teaches them body movements that go along with those products (skip counting), in the form of "dances" where students stand and gesture (hands over their heads, arms in a windmill, touching the knees, pointing in one direction, etc.) as they go through the progression for the eights (8, 16, 24, 32, 40, 48). Introducing them one at a time, Bowerman teaches her fourth graders a different dance for the fours, the sixes, the sevens, and so forth. The dances are perfect for transitions and breaks throughout the course of the school year, and they reinforce math concepts in the process.

When a video crew showed up at Bowerman's door one day, she put the kids through their paces. I had occasion to view these tapes, and I can report that two things were readily apparent: First, these students had clearly used the gestures to memorize the progressions, and they did not miss a beat. Second, it was apparent that they loved doing the dances. For the sevens (touchdown and extra point), all the gestures had to do with football, including a touchdown signal for the number 70. The whole sevens sequence was done in the form of one, long, continuous cheer.

Again, Bowerman clearly understands that kids have to be physically involved in their own learning, and her fourth graders continually show their appreciation for being able to do so. Because she took the time to discuss with them the importance of physical activity as it relates to learning, they know how something they love doing can also help them academically. In Chapter 8, we'll return to Bowerman's classroom for a look at how she harnesses the power of student reflection in support of continuous improvement.

Students Need to Know It Is Okay to Be Wrong or Make Mistakes

To grow is to take risks. To learn involves moving out of one's comfort zone. To improve is to make mistakes and learn from them. Students must feel comfortable moving out of their own comfort zones. In a nation obsessed with testing, we are so concerned about getting the *right answers* that we have created a school culture where getting ahead may be less about growing academically or intellectually than it is about finding those answers. According to Tileston (2004), we must create classrooms where the stress is low to moderate and the challenge is high, so that students "know it is all right if they do not know all the answers" (p. 30). The reality is that students will not perform well in an environment where they are afraid that not having the right answers on demand will lead to them being singled out or ridiculed.

Mistakes are the lifeblood of progress. No organization or individual has ever moved far down the improvement highway without making—and learning from—mistakes. Teachers need to help students understand that making mistakes is both human and expected. The best business organizations in the world seek feedback from customers, so the mistakes the companies make can be surfaced, analyzed, and used to improve quality and performance. In an environment where students are afraid to make mistakes, teacher feedback may be seen as criticism rather than what it is—a chance to move from where the student is now to where he wants to be. I would go so far as to say that it is not the mistakes we do find that cause problems; it is those we do *not* find that impair progress. Coaches count on mistakes being surfaced in order to make necessary adjustments; teachers need to make students understand that surfacing mistakes in any educational product is not only necessary but also desirable. The important relationship between the making of mistakes and the giving of feedback should be discussed at length during the first week of school.

Students Appreciate the Efficient Use of Time

In many classrooms, a good deal of time is wasted in giving directions, transitioning from one activity to another, collecting papers, distributing handouts, or encouraging—or participating in—distracting side conversations. Once again, this goes to process, not content. One very effective way to save time is to go visual when possible. Something as seemingly simple as asking students to turn to page 76 can get ugly if Eddie didn't hear you. His hand is bound to go up as he notices that there is activity all around him and simultaneously realizes that he has no idea what is going on. If the page to which he needs to turn is visually displayed on the screen in 44-point Times New Roman, it is pretty difficult for him to make the wrong move or to sit there with a puzzled expression on his face.

Teachers can also make it a point to transition quickly from task to task within the classroom setting; work will expand to fit the time allotted, and I have seen many students transition a whole lot more slowly if they are given that option. Teachers can work with students during the first month of school on transitioning quickly, without wasted effort or time. Getting into the classroom, getting down to work; getting into pairs or groups, getting back to their seats, getting everything cleaned up, and getting lined up or otherwise ready to go—all that should happen quickly and smoothly. It will only happen, however, if a teacher's expectations here are high, and if he or she refuses to accept slow when fast is the standard. If students infer that standards relating to the use of time in the classroom are lacking or inconsistent, it is they who will determine how long various transitions take, not the teacher.

Students Like to Laugh

Active classrooms, by my definition, are places where (appropriate) laughter is common. I am not speaking of the kind of laughter that comes as a result of sarcasm or put-downs on the part of students or teachers. I am talking about the kind of healthy laughter that follows a funny story, a humorous personal anecdote, or any number of occurrences during the course of a school day. As a teacher, I would often latch onto something I said or did and turn it into a running gag for the rest of the class period, week, or school year. Self-depreciative humor used by a teacher is a way of telling students you take your job seriously; you take the content seriously; but you don't take yourself too seriously. Laughter is healthy. According to Smith (2005), it "contributes to enhancing the immune system and increasing natural disease-fighting cells" (p. 162). Supporting laughter in support of learning, Smith continues, "People are better able to deal with cognitive challenge when they approach the challenge through shared laughter with others" (p. 162). I have found that if adult participants in my workshops are made to laugh before they begin discussing something with each other, they enter into the spirit of the thing much more quickly and completely. Shared laughter is indeed a powerful tool.

Students Appreciate Consistency

There can be little doubt that students value a teacher who is consistent in his approach to discipline, grading, and classroom procedures. Tileston (2004) reminds teachers that they should "never ignore poor behavior; to do so is to send a signal to your students that order and discipline is not important" (p. 30). If students are not clear as to how teachers arrived at a particular letter grade, or if the assigning of grades appears to be inconsistent, they will be understandably confused and irritated. If classroom procedures are explained and then not followed, this will once again result in confusion. Teachers who are not consistent as it pertains to process will most certainly run into problems within weeks after school begins in the summer or fall.

Jones (2007) speaks to the issue of consistency by pointing out that one is either consistent, or one is inconsistent. "There is nothing in between. There is no such thing as 'pretty consistent' or 'very consistent' or 'extremely consistent'" (p. 186). Jones goes on to say that teachers need to deal with small disruptions in the classroom before they get bigger; he points out that it is small disruptions that "account for the lion's share of lost learning time and teacher stress" (p. 187). My experience is that teachers who are inconsistent in their handling of kids talking or otherwise misbehaving are in for a long school year. Teachers need to decide how they will handle these classroom disruptions, and then they need to follow through on a consistent basis in a consistent manner. Out-of-control classrooms are demotivators for kids who are serious about the business of learning.

Students Enjoy a Change of State

The most successful classrooms I have visited over the years are those where teachers understand the importance of changing their students' physical and mental state on a frequent basis. If students are seated, have them stand. If they are working individually, have them pair up. If they are moving from one place to another in the classroom, play some music. If they have been reading for a few minutes, have them stand and chat for a minute or so in pairs or groups. If they are doing one thing, have them do another thing. According to Allen (2010), this allows the brain to refocus, and "for a brief period of time, it will feel like something new, a condition in which the brain tends to be in a heightened level of awareness" (p. 36). Anyone who teaches a 90-minute block in high school can see to it that state changes occur every 10 to 12 minutes.

Teachers also need to be able to "read" their students. When working with adults in the workshop setting, I always go into action with a plan. At any point during the session, I know exactly what should happen next. Nevertheless, there are occasions when I see the kind of body language that tells me I have gone over my 10-minute allocation for that activity, or I deduce that I need to substitute one activity for another in order to provide a more-complete change of state. This adjustment, along with some upbeat music for the transition, gets me the results I want—participants who are energized and engaged at every turn. My suggestion to secondary teachers is that they change the physical or mental state of their students every 10 minutes or so. For elementary teachers, 10 minutes is probably too long. Again, teachers need to learn to read the audience and make adjustments accordingly.

The Middle Years

For teachers working on teams at the middle-school level, I suggest that a good deal of time be spent in the summer working out consistencies in grading, testing (so tests in different subject areas are not given on the same day), approach to discipline, and even procedures. If eighth graders on the Phoenix Team know that regardless of what classroom they are in today, the drill will be the same, they will adjust to team standards and norms more quickly. No matter what classroom they are in on a given day, students can count on consistency when it comes to procedures. During the summer, or, if there is time, during teacher week, teams can also meet and brainstorm ways to change states in their classrooms. The most exciting and productive two years of my teaching career came as part of a seventh-grade inclusion team. A good deal of my energy during those years came from the collaborative efforts of our team members to maintain consistency, improve efficiency, and facilitate progress for our students.

Final Thoughts

Teachers can do a great deal to ensure that their students want to be the first ones at the bus stop in the morning and the last ones out of the classroom at day's end. In fact, I would say a great vision statement for any school might be "We won't rest until every student wants to be the first one in and the last one out." This would be hard to measure, maybe, but easy to understand. The single thread that I believe runs through truly active, engaging classrooms, is a desire to be there on the part of students of any grade level. When kids come home and want to share what went on in school that day, this should serve as an indicator to parents that good things are happening during the school day. When teachers love coming to school every day, it is a sign that things are going well in the classroom. When administrators hear much laughter when teachers get together, it may be indicative of a school filled with happy campers of all age levels.

We can be serious about education and have fun in the classroom. We can have fun in the classroom while kids get a great education. My final observation is that classrooms that run on all cylinders are fueled by a commitment to children and their progress, a dedication to lifelong learning . . . and a sense of humor. I often ask teachers to share with a partner or group a story about a favorite teacher. As I walk around and listen to the conversations, I hear stories that, taken in the aggregate, tell me much about the role of humor in the pantheon of great teachers. In the stories, and laughter, these teachers share with others, I am reminded that the journey through our school years ought to be eventful, productive, and rewarding, and that hallways and classrooms ought to echo with the sound of laughter.

Feedback and checking for understanding are critical pieces of the educational puzzle, and in Chapter 5 we'll delve into the structure and uses of both.

5

Feedback
Pure and Simple

Early in my career as a secondary history teacher, I assigned homework to my students almost every night. At the end of an exciting [sic] lecture on the causes of the Civil War or the rise of labor unions, I would inevitably point to that place on the blackboard where I had recorded the assignment. Because I was textbook driven, I normally had students answer the end-of-section questions for submission the following day. The next day, I collected the assignments, and I took great pride in the fact that I gave students credit for getting the assignment in and—mostly—correct. Sloppy work did not receive the checkmark that was my currency for a job completed on time. I explained to the students that the checkmarks became part of the grade, an explanation that in my mind was sure to motivate their completion of the homework on a regular, or at least semiregular, basis. As fall gave way to winter, I struggled to come up with an explanation as to why the quantity of completed homework was dwindling, along with the quality. I fussed, I fumed, and I played the blame game: The students didn't want to learn; the textbook was too difficult; parents were not making the kids work hard enough; not enough time was spent on homework. In the end, all those checkmarks on completed assignments did not seem to be doing the trick; their grades were inevitably affected, and my disappointment was transparent and profound.

In those early years, my approach to homework, quizzes, and tests was summative in nature. I assigned homework and administered regular assessments in order to provide entries in my grade book. By the time my students received the results from all these end-of-whatever-we-just-finished assessments, we had moved on. The checkmark, the letter grade, and/or the percentage recorded on countless pieces of student work provided me with something to record. It provided students with a sort of postmortem on a given chapter or unit. An actual postmortem may provide the medical establishment with useful data and important answers to intriguing questions; it does little for the deceased. Summative assessments can certainly inform instruction in a way that helps teachers improve their own performance, and for that reason they have value; but there has to be something else made available to students that informs, encourages, and assists their own steady and relentless progress. That something is meaningful, useful, and timely feedback.

Once my students realized I was not going to give them meaningful feedback of any sort on their homework papers, they simply stopped performing. Students who *did* value letter grades went through the motions and thus assured their grades would not deteriorate as the year progressed. Others made the calculation that the price of not doing the homework on a regular basis was not high enough to merit continuing to hand it in. My homework completion rate was high every September—until it became apparent that completing the assignments did not seem to provide much in the way of feedback. Some of them, no doubt, handed it in to please me; others may have been driven to complete regular assignments by someone at home.

Over the years, I have observed that students who continue to get back papers, tests, and quizzes with low grades simply continue on that downward spiral. Students who are *competitive* when it comes to grades will ask the inevitable question: "Will this be on the test?" The clear implication here is that he or she is not really interested unless the information *is* on the test. We don't help as teachers when we say, as I once said with great frequency, "Come on now. This is going to be on the test!" By saying that, I deeply discounted anything of value that would *not* be on the next test or quiz. By putting that squarely on the table, I made *everything* about the next test or quiz.

As a history teacher who loved the subject, I wanted students to pursue the study of United States history with my fervor and dedication. Unfortunately, I approached it from the top down rather than from the bottom up. That is, I put the letter or percentage grade on a pedestal and told my students that the most important thing was to get the A. With a B student, the sum total of my advice was to raise that B to an A. My love of the subject matter was overshadowed by my insistence on the attainment of an ever-higher letter grade.

If we look at this from the bottom up, beginning with learning and not with an emphasis on conquering the grade summit, students can learn the information, improve their own performance—and they will take care of any tests that come their way as a matter of course. I have been in classrooms where students concentrate on improving their own skills in any number of areas and actually look forward to the state tests at the end of the year; they do this because they know they are capable and confident learners.

When Collaboration Replaces Competition

A few years ago, a very successful football team failed to go undefeated for the season. They lost one game—the *last* game. Yet, an announcer declared them losers. The locker room was a somber place for a team that lost only one game. "This is what happens," says Deci (1995), "when we turn everything into a contest where there is only one winner, in which winning matters more than playing well or being a good sport" (p. 69). The common wisdom in sports is that there is only one winner. We can't afford that to be the case in education.

I once spent a class period in a high-school science classroom where the expectation on the part of the teacher was that anything less than an A grade was unacceptable. There was virtually no competition for the grades, because it was assumed that all her students would keep going until they attained a high level of performance. Those high-school juniors collaborated willingly, taught each other, and sought necessary help from the teacher consistently in an effort to increase understanding—and the grades rose during the semester. Students charted their own progress on run charts; they charted the progress of the entire class; and as grades went up or down, they spent time looking for root causes in an effort to understand what was wrong and what needed to be done to improve. Their attitude was excellent, and several of them informed me that they preferred this more-formative approach to the summative practices in their other classes.

The teacher in that science class understood that competition can have a negative effect on collaboration if everyone is looking to kick everyone else off the island. What her students communicated to me near the end of the class period that day was that their goal was to help their classmates improve, not to climb ahead in an individual effort to get to the top over the [figurative] bodies of their peers. Kohn (1999) laments, "learning doesn't stand a chance when the point is to keep up with, or triumph over, other students" (p. 37). That high-school science teacher understood this, *and she enlisted the help of every student in her class in helping the entire class improve on a daily basis.* This was so integrated into process that I was in the classroom for a few minutes before I figured out who the teacher was; it was actually a *student* who welcomed me and showed me what they were doing. In this case, competition had been replaced with collaboration; feedback for students who needed help was available at every turn from those who understood *this* concept or *that* topic more clearly.

One elementary teacher, in an effort to improve the reading level of his students, took a collaborative approach and combined individual reading levels into an average for the whole class. He used a transparency displaying a bar graph to show his students where they were in terms of their collective reading level as of October. He then had them set a class goal for where they wanted to be come January.

Each month, he revisited the bar graph, so they could gauge their collective progress. In November and December, they improved steadily. He frequently had students brainstorm ways to improve their own individual reading level in support of the group effort. He provided feedback and encouragement to individual students as to how they could improve on an individual basis (each student had his or her individual goal as well). Come January, he revealed that they had indeed met their class goal for that month; he reports there was a great deal of celebrating, hand clapping, high fiving, and cheering. By progressing individually, *his elementary students were contributing to the continuous-improvement goals of the entire class.* They got excited about contributing to an overall-improvement process on the way to a collective goal.

The Purpose and Nature of Feedback

If our focus is on learning, as well as on the improvement of skill level and performance, then it is critical that students understand where they are, where they are going, and what it will take to get there over time. Popham (2008) affirms that *comparative* feedback (where students are in relation to each other) is less effective than *descriptive* feedback, which "indicates what students can currently do and what they need to do in order to achieve a target curricular aim or master an en route building block related to that aim" (p. 114). Comparative feedback invites competition and discourages collaboration; it is possible to harness the *collective* power of the group in order to improve everyone's performance. At the same time, students can improve along an absolute scale, receiving feedback that assists them in their journey.

Feedback should be clear and specific, according to Brookhart (2008); and writing, "Good work!" or, "Good job!" on a student's paper tells him little. The student may feel good at the time, but if the goal is to help him improve his writing, for example, then it may be more helpful to the student to make a notation in the margin that says, "Your use of adjectives in this paragraph helps clarify its meaning." Circling the adjectives helps clarify the teacher's comment, and the specificity of the notation and the circling of the adjectives leaves little doubt as to what the student has done that is right on the money. If the adjectives are lacking, on the other hand, the margin note can say, "Using a couple of adjectives here might provide clarity." This tells the student that when he moves to the next draft, the inclusion of adjectives might improve his effort. *The student can do something with this,* and Brookhart points out that this gives students a sense of control over their learning that is "true self-efficacy. It is the foundation of motivation for learning" (p. 35). Saying, "Super job!" on the student's paper is a temporary feel-good move, but it provides no traction for improvement.

Vatterott (2009) asserts that the role of homework should be *formative* in nature, not summative. That is, rather than being the last word, feedback should be given in a manner that allows students to make adjustments in their work, thus improving both the product and the skill set used to create it. Marzano, Pickering, and Pollock (2001) conclude, "the best feedback appears to involve an explanation as to what is accurate and what is inaccurate in terms of student responses. In addition, asking students to keep working on a task until they succeed appears to enhance achievement" (p. 96). This feedback is corrective in nature, and it keeps students informed as to where they are now, at the same time letting them know what needs to be changed in order to make progress.

Timeliness and Hitting the Reset Button

Feedback should also be timely. Papers, tests, quizzes, and other completed assignments need to be returned quickly. This means teachers need to plan carefully, not overloading themselves or their students with so many assignments that it is impossible for students to get them done and equally impossible to get the feedback on the assignments back in a timely fashion. Over the years, one of the biggest complaints from students with whom I have spoken is that they will work hard on something and, once it is handed in, it seems to disappear into a black hole. Creating a schedule for assignments and summative assessments that does not overload students and teachers alike is a function of planning.

When teachers get seriously behind, they feel overwhelmed; I have known teachers who have been almost literally buried in mountains of paperwork and unfinished business. Students who see this mountain grow steadily higher on the teacher's desk or on the top of a couple of cabinets are likely to wonder what is going on. My suggestion is that if this happens, teachers should stop, apologize, and have a frank discussion with students, explaining that it is necessary to hold off on homework for a week (they may not mind) until the decks are cleared and assignments already completed have been returned. Catching up benefits everyone, and students will appreciate the honesty. Once things are back to normal, teachers can adjust the assignment flow so that it does not happen again.

It is also helpful if teachers can get some sort of feedback from students as to how relatively easy or difficult a particular homework assignment was. Vatterott (2009) suggests that students use colored stickers to indicate their level of understanding. A green sticker would indicate they understand; a yellow sticker would communicate uncertainty to the teacher; a red sticker would tell teachers that the student simply did not understand the assignment (p. 117). If the teacher is using corrective feedback, along with the stickers, then the feedback is flowing both ways in a way that will benefit teacher and students alike.

One of the problems with homework, as we saw earlier in the chapter, is that feedback from the teacher may be lacking. The homework comes in; and from the student's perspective, it either disappears or appears again with a sticker or general remark, along the lines of "Good work." If, on the other hand, the homework is given less frequently, but is then made part of the following day's lesson, it may be seen to have more value. If, as Brookhart (2008) suggests, teachers demonstrate to students that they read the homework by sharing something the homework revealed about the basic level of understanding related to a particular topic, then students might see that the teacher places value on the homework.

Brookhart (2008) uses the example of a homework assignment that dealt with the earth's rotation on its axis and its revolution around the sun. After "restating for the class that their learning goal was to understand how planets move," the teacher could explain that they appeared to understand "revolution better than rotation" (p. 55). Not only does this provide a departure point for discussion and correcting misunderstandings, it also tells students that the teacher has actually read and analyzed the homework. The teacher who backs this up by including specific written feedback on the homework paper is investing in a higher level of return on homework assignments.

My sense is that giving two assignments per week—as opposed to four—but clearing the decks to spend more time in reading them and providing feedback, will result in a higher rate of return and better quality. During that first week of school with students, a teacher can have a frank discussion about homework and commit right up front and in writing (so parents understand what is going on) to improving the quantity and quality of the feedback. If students know out of the gate that the teacher is *serious about what they turn in and what she gives back,* they may be more likely to make a commitment of their own in terms of the quantity and quality of their work.

Road Maps Are Useful

When I hit 30, I also hit the road. As a sales representative for a national company, I traveled all over 21 Ohio counties. I'd have been lost without a road map in that pre-GPS era, and the atlas I had in my car was well thumbed and much appreciated. If I was going from our house in Bellefontaine to Springfield, I could mark my progress and estimate how many more miles—and minutes—I had to go in order to keep my appointment. I did not have to check with anyone because of the map, and it gave me confidence—even in an unfamiliar sales territory. Detours revealed themselves, but I had the map, and I could find a new route without difficulty. With time on my hands, I could even visit a potential customer several miles off the beaten path, and that was okay, too—I had my map. As long as my destination was clear, I was in good shape.

In education today, we not only possess local curricular standards but we also have the ubiquitous state standards—and we have them in several subject areas. An elementary teacher must be familiar with more than one set of standards, and new teachers in particular will be forgiven if they are confused and, at times, overwhelmed. Imagine, then, what students must feel like as they try to navigate the highways and byways of English, math, social studies, and science standards that drive instruction today. The job of teachers, in conjunction with administrators and district-level curriculum specialists, is to "unpack" the standards at every grade and subject level, in order to create a sort of road map for students.

One way for teachers to provide students with their own road map is to construct simple, easy-to-use student checklists against which students can measure progress. Student checklists, according to Burke (2006), consist of a "mini-item analysis where the teacher 'deconstructs' or 'dissects' the abstract standard and classifies and sequences the discrete skills into manageable steps" (p. 102). The emphasis is on providing "user-friendly guidelines" that are "often written in question format to guide students through each step of the process" (p. 102). Checklist in hand, students can proceed toward a destination, safe in the knowledge that nothing will be left out or unintentionally overlooked. Detours may present themselves, and obstacles may delay progress—but a student with a checklist can feel every bit as confident as I did with my road map many years ago in those 21 unfamiliar Ohio counties.

Yvonne Stroud—Grade 7 Math

Stroud has a strong background in special education, and while she has many students who are not afraid to ask for help, there are some students who are simply not willing to do so. One of Stroud's struggling students, and one of those unwilling to ask for assistance, responded well on a checklist for a geometry task. Stroud noticed this willingness to use the checklist, and the student subsequently received a rare perfect score on a performance-task assessment.

Stroud has also found that many students ask more detailed and specific questions because of the checklists. Because they all have the same checklist, they tend to ask each other for help, should they need it, before going to Stroud. She had concluded that the checklists help her students to become more independent and interdependent learners.

Figures 5.1 and 5.2 show two examples of Stroud's math checklists.

Notice that the decimals checklist (Figure 5.2) is based on the state math standard that says students *will be able to use fractions, decimals, and percents interchangeably*. With a Yes column and a No column, students can navigate these questions easily and seek help from peers or Stroud if necessary. Stroud's goal is to create a whole series of checklists for math, as references her students can utilize in the classroom. The most important thing is that Stroud shifts the work from herself to her students; it is they who are in charge of their own road maps here, and Stroud can concentrate on where the weaknesses appear as she monitors their use of the checklists.

Figure 5.1 Coordinating-Translations Checklist

Grade 7—Students will demonstrate understanding of transformations.	Yes 0	No 1
a. Demonstrate understanding of translations, dilations, rotations, reflections, and relate symmetry to appropriate transformations.		
b. Given a figure in the coordinate plane, determine the coordinates resulting from a translation, dilation, rotation, or reflection.		
Plot a creative, original polygon (preimage)	**Did you**	
• Create an original polygon? *Polygon: plane shape having three or more straight sides*		
• Label the vertices of your original polygon? *Vertex: point where surfaces meet-corner; example:* A, B, C		
• Chart the coordinates of each vertex? *Example: (4, –6) (x-coordinate, y-coordinate)*		
1. Create a congruent image from original at $(x + 4, y)$	**Did you**	
• Translate (slide) the original polygon to its new coordinates?		
• Label the vertices of your new polygon? *Example:* A', B', C'		
• Chart the coordinates of each new vertex?		
2. Create congruent image from original at $(x, y - 3)$	**Did you**	
• Translate (slide) the original polygon to its new coordinates?		
• Label the vertices of your new polygon?		
• Chart the coordinates of each new vertex?		
3. Create congruent image from original at $(x - 4, y + 1)$	**Did you**	
• Translate (slide) the original polygon to its new coordinates?		
• Label the vertices of your new polygon?		
• Chart the coordinates of each new vertex?		
4. Provide descriptions of each translation's position, shape, and size	**Did you**	
• Tell what happens to an image when you add units to the original x-coordinates $(x + c, y)$?		
• Tell what happens to an image when you subtract units from the original x-coordinates $(x - c, y)$?		
• Tell what happens to an image when you add units to the original y-coordinates $(x, y + c)$?		
• Tell what happens to an image when you subtract units from the original y-coordinates $(x, y - c)$?		

SOURCE: Yvonne Stroud. Used with permission.

Figure 5.2 Computing With Decimals

Grade 6—Students will use fractions, decimals, and percents interchangeably.	Yes	No
Addition	**Did you**	
• Line up the decimal points?		
• Add the numbers as you would for any whole numbers?		
• Move the decimal straight down in the answer?		
• Add zeros as placeholders when necessary?		
Subtraction	**Did you**	
• Line up the decimal points?		
• Subtract the numbers as you would for any whole numbers?		
• Move the decimal straight down in the answer?		
• Add zeros as placeholders when necessary?		
Multiplication	**Did you**	
• Multiply the numbers as you would any whole numbers?		
• Count the number of decimal places in the factors?		
• Move the decimal that many places from the left in the answer?		
Division	**Did you**	
• Move the decimal point in the divisor to the right to make it a whole number?		
• Move the decimal point in the dividend to the right the same number of places?		
• Divide as you would any whole number?		
• Move the decimal point straight up in the quotient?		

SOURCE: Yvonne Stroud. Used with permission.

Rubrics

Checklists tied to state standards can "help students organize and complete their work in a sequential order..." (Burke, 2009, p. 92). Burke goes on to say that a checklist (2009), "can be easily converted to the rubric by adding descriptors of quality at each level" (p. 93). The checklist informs students as to what needs to be done when; the rubric provides signposts in the continuous-improvement journey as it relates to a specific activity or task. The key here is *clarity*. Students often have a somewhat hazy notion as to what a teacher expects as it relates to an assignment or project. The combination of a checklist and a rubric serves to dispel any ambiguity; it also keeps teachers from having to answer the question, "What do we need to do, and how good is good?" over and over again.

Jenny Sue Flannagan, a university-level assistant professor, works with prospective teachers in the area of science education. Flannagan understands that although the development of an extensive rubric takes a good deal of *her* time up front, it invariably pays off down the road. It helps her focus on what she wants; it helps her university students operate during the semester, knowing exactly what they need to do to produce quality work. By taking the time to develop a rubric, Flannagan frontloads for success.

Jenny Sue Flannagan—University Assistant Professor

In assisting her students in the development of quality lesson plans in science, Flannagan first spends a good deal of time working with them on the importance of inquiry in science education. In fact, this is a main focus of the course, so she includes this in an extensive rubric, part of which is reproduced in Figure 5.3. Realizing that most of the students with whom she works will be dealing with the Virginia Standards of Learning, she makes certain this is included as well. Having stressed the importance and effectiveness of formative assessments in their classrooms, Flannagan includes that in the rubric.

Figure 5.3 Science Education Rubric (Partial)

Lesson Plan	Exceeds Expectations: 3	Meets Expectations: 2	Does Not Meet Expectations: 1
a. Objectives	Objectives are listed and are supported by lesson activities; all are appropriate for the lesson.	Objectives are listed; student has a couple of extra objectives or too few objectives; a few seem somewhat inappropriate for the lesson.	Objectives are not listed; way too few or many objectives; several seem inappropriate for the lesson.

(Continued)

(Continued)

Lesson Plan	Exceeds Expectations: 3	Meets Expectations: 2	Does Not Meet Expectations: 1
b. State Standards	Lesson addresses all standards that are listed; no standards are missing; incorporates standards into real-life examples; utilizes standards in more than one content area.	The lesson only addresses some standards that it purports to address and/or some standards are missing; utilizes standards in more than one content area.	The lesson fails to adequately address the standards listed, and several of the standards are missing.
c. Explanation/ Alignment of Lesson Activities	The explanation of the lesson is easy to understand; description of activities are clear and detailed enough so that someone else could run the lesson; activities are aligned to the objectives and would help students to answer the essential questions.	The explanation is somewhat difficult to understand; it needs more details for someone else to lead instruction; some activities are not appropriately aligned to objectives/standards.	The explanation is not orderly; it is hard to follow; it has too little detail; the activities are not appropriate for lesson; they are not aligned to objectives/ standards.
d. Use of Instructional Strategies	Strategies used in the lesson help the lesson to be more inquiry based; it is clear the strategies are used to help support one or more of the essential features of inquiry.	Strategies used in the lesson help the lesson to be more inquiry based; however, they only support one essential feature of inquiry.	Strategies used in the lesson are used only as the primary mode of information dissemination or note taking.
e. Assessment	The lesson uses a variety of formative assessments that will provide the teacher with data indicating who is mastering ideas and skills and who may need more assistance.	The lesson includes some formative assessment.	The lesson includes no assessment tools.

Lesson Plan	Exceeds Expectations: 3	Meets Expectations: 2	Does Not Meet Expectations: I
f. Resources	Sources of lesson-plan ideas clearly identified so that someone else could locate the sources; a variety of sources were used to write the lesson plan; the lesson uses multiple nonpaper resources (media, audiovisual, etc.); handouts are provided.	Sources of lesson-plan ideas are clearly identified so that someone else could locate the sources; a variety of sources were used to write lesson plan; the lesson uses a nonpaper resource (media, audiovisual, etc.).	Source of lesson-plan ideas clearly identified so that someone else could locate the source; a variety of sources were used to write lesson plan.
g. Inquiry-Based	The lesson is designed to meet three or more of the essential features of inquiry.	The lesson meets only one to two essential features of inquiry.	The lesson is not designed to include any essential features of inquiry.

Her university students find it helpful to have something they can refer to at any time as they work on their lesson plans. The whole notion of quality as it relates to the creation of those science lesson plans is clear and totally unambiguous because Flannagan took the time to create a road map for success in the form of a tightly composed rubric.

Another Signpost on the Continuous-Improvement Highway

Another way in which students can check and reflect on their own progress is through the use of bar graphs or run charts. If a student is working to improve a specific skill over time (writing, for example), it is helpful to provide signposts that tell a student where he is along his own continuous-improvement highway. One data point showing a specific score for that week tells the student where he is; the results for the next three or four weeks recorded on a bar graph or run chart provide that student with a trend. If the trend over several weeks is up, the student knows that whatever he is doing on his own behalf in that skill area is working. If the trend is downward, this tells him that what he is doing is not enough, or something different may be required in order to reverse the trend.

It is not enough, however, to have the students record the data week after week without putting in place a process to *use the data* to their benefit. They must be taught to analyze the data. The run chart or bar graph itself is not the end product; it is the means to an end. Teachers need to work with students individually and at the classroom level to enable them to understand what the trend lines may mean. I observed a high-school class where the students not only kept individual run charts but the teacher also took the average of their grades and posted it on the wall. She then led them in a discussion about what might have caused the latest grade average to decline or increase. Either way, she wanted to know what may have caused the change, and they brainstormed possible reasons for the results—up, down, or no change at all.

It is one thing for students to have a general idea that they are getting better at something; it is another thing entirely to be able to look at the results on a bar graph or run chart and then *take the time to reflect on their own progress.* Visuals have impact. Students and teachers alike can see by looking at the chart whether or not they are making progress. Also, students must be taught to see data as data—and not as judgment. The new data point on the chart or graph simply tells them where they are. It is up to them, *at the teacher's direction,* to figure out what to do in order to move the next data point in the direction they wish it to go. Feedback is just feedback. It is not good or bad, and it is not judgmental; it is simply an indication of where the student is now. The key questions become Where am I currently in my own continuous-improvement journey? If the trend line is going down, how did that happen? If the trend line is going up, how did that happen? Where do I want to go next, and what is the best way for me to get there? Do I simply do more of the same—whatever that is—or do I need to introduce change in order to move the trend line in the direction I wish it to go? Is there anything or anyone who can help me succeed?

In Chapter 4, we visited the classroom of fourth-grade teacher Becky Bowerman. Through the use of physical activity in the form of "dances," Bowerman harnessed the power of physical activity to help her students learn their multiplication tables. She also uses reflection and individual student data in order to accelerate their learning.

Becky Bowerman—Grade 4 Teacher

Each student in Bowerman's class is responsible for maintaining an individual-data notebook. On Friday of each week, students take a 100-problem timed test. When the tests are scored, Bowerman enters the data into a spreadsheet. Using the spreadsheet, she can then provide each student with a bar graph that tracks individual progress over time. Weekly, students are responsible for analyzing the graphs in an attempt to figure out how they can shift a downward trend the other way, or accelerate slow but continuous progress. Bowerman brainstorms with them ways they might improve their scores from week to week.

One of her students indicated that in his first weekly test, he scored a 31. Working with a computer program, he improved his score in one week to a 44. Not satisfied, he decided another change was in order; he began using flash cards, the use of which brought his grade up to a 68. This considerable improvement of 24 points resulted in some complacency on his part, and he dropped two points to a 66. In his own words, he "got a bit cocky," and took his foot off the proverbial gas pedal. Realizing that his slight drop was due to a lack of effort on his part, he went back to the flash cards, invested more of his own time—and raised his score to 84. Encouraged, and with enough data points and analysis to show him the efficacy of hard work, his graph showed an improvement of 15 points, from 84 to 99.

Bowerman's students also set individual goals, and they must come up with a written plan that states exactly how they intend to meet that goal. The goals, plans, and graphs are shared with parents, who have a chance to add comments. Students will often compare charts and discuss with each other ways to improve. Sometimes, it is simply a matter of deciding that doing nothing between one Friday test and the next does not really help reach a stated goal. After coming to grips with a bar graph that showed a decline in scores in weeks five and six, one of Bowerman's students realized she "couldn't learn by magic," so she studied; and her score went up 14 points, from 75 to 89. Faced with a goal on one hand, and a lack of progress toward that goal on the other, she simply decided that nothing changes if nothing changes.

Bowerman also tracks the progress of the entire class over time. During the first nine-week grading period, the average score on these weekly math tests increased 52.9%, and the average score stood at 91.2%. This is remarkable progress, and Bowerman attributes this success to the system she has in place. This system encourages responsibility on the part of students who are taught to begin from a starting point, set goals, analyze their progress (or lack thereof), and put in place specific, concrete measures that will accelerate the rate of growth over time.

In Figure 5.4, one of Bowerman's students looked at the first data point (a score of 21) and was not pleased with her own performance.

Figure 5.4 One Student's Weekly Multiplication Scores

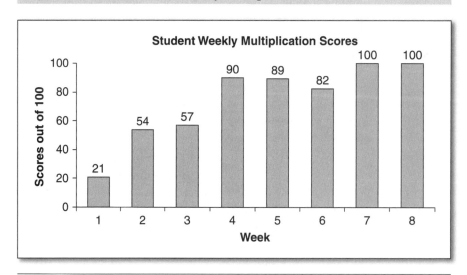

SOURCE: Rebecca Bowerman. Used with Permission.

Part of her original contract (a component of her individual plan) had called for studying 20 minutes per day. She and her mother signed the contract, and she went to work. Using Internet programs and flash cards, she improved by 33 points in week two. After a week in which she improved by only 3 points, she went back to the flash cards and computer programs, and her score jumped to a 90 in week four. After two more weeks of holding her own or going down, she made a commitment to study a little bit more each day. Week seven brought a perfect score, a feat that was repeated in week eight. Importantly, she credited the graph with showing her the results of studying and not studying.

As students proceed through the nine-week grading period, they have the opportunity to compare their grades against the class average. Bowerman's students loved seeing the class average improve week by week, with only one small dip from week four to week five. They were also able to compare their own scores with the class average, and the student whose graph appears above was happy when she surpassed the class average in week four. Figure 5.5 shows this comparison. It is important to note that students are not competing against each other; they are working to improve their own score, and they can compare their own scores with the class average, but they celebrate their own progress even as they celebrate the upward movement of the entire class.

Figure 5.5 Student Score Juxtaposed With Class Score

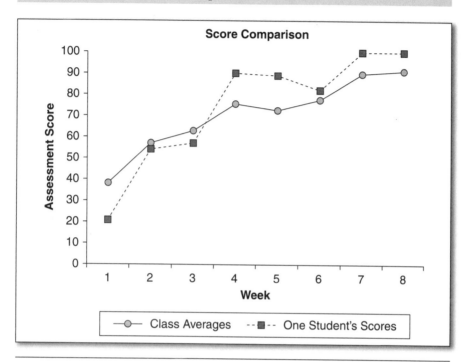

SOURCE: Rebecca Bowerman. Used with Permission.

Final Thoughts

Teachers need to provide time for students to reflect, individually or as a group, on what they need to do in order to improve performance. Gregory and Parry (1998) tell us, "students must learn to reflect and to analyze what they have or have not learned, what misconceptions they have, and what actions they need to take next" (p. 214). Students who learn to analyze and adjust have learned a valuable life skill that will serve them well in the workplace and in life in general. Feedback should be highly descriptive, and it should not be negative. The important thing here is for a student, using a checklist or rubric, for example, to be able to determine where he is on his own personal continuous-improvement journey. The teacher's role here is one of process facilitator and coach, but the student ought to be expected and fully able to read the map.

In Chapter 6, we'll discover what makes teachers tick and classrooms click.

6

When Teachers Tick and Classrooms Click

After viewing a short video clip, Dana Hand's third graders stand to the sound of some upbeat music, find a partner, and get ready to share what they learned. Hand always provides a twist to the activity. In this case, she literally showers the room with adjectives on pieces of paper. The kids scramble to pick up words like happy, funny, jubilant, nervous, surprised, soft, *or* loud. *They share with classmates what they learned in the tone of voice described by the adjectives. Then, Hand collects the cards and draws one at random. If she draws the word* angry, *for example, the student who was paired with the "angry" student might say, "Johnny angrily reported that the most important piece of information in the video is that simple machines make work easier." The student doing the reporting uses that angry voice, just as Johnny did. The kids love it and know they must pay attention during the video and during the reporting that takes place in pairs once the video is over. This classroom clicks, and Dana Hand choreographs the interaction in a way that keeps the process flowing smoothly, harnessing the natural energy of her third graders.*

Over the years, I have enjoyed my journey through the educational landscape as a substitute teacher, secondary teacher, curriculum coordinator, organizational-development specialist, trainer, teacher coach, and author. Visiting hundreds of classrooms has allowed me to take the "balcony view" in an attempt to assist teachers in their own continuous-improvement efforts. Along the way, I have come to several basic conclusions about what makes teachers and classrooms inviting, vibrant, and ultimately effective.

Shifting Students From Passive to Active

I had many college classes in history (my major) where we as graduate students (less so in undergraduate courses) were able to discuss at length this theme, or that concept, or those events. I enjoyed those courses for the simple fact that we could proceed at a more leisurely pace than in undergraduate courses with large numbers of students. I learned much more when we were able to discuss, process, grapple with, argue about, infer, analyze, and defend as a regular part of doing business in that classroom. I particularly enjoyed one political-science class where the professor continually asked questions, after which he would give us time to think about our responses. He answered our questions with more questions; he was, as became apparent, more interested in helping us develop critical-thinking skills than in us finding the "right answers" to complex questions. Thinking back, I contrast that course with another in which the professor read in a monotone from a thick sheaf of yellowed notes, as he chain-smoked his way through a 90-minute class.

Actually, I love listening to lectures on tape or CD today, and I usually have one or two in my car to enjoy while driving long distances. Part of the beauty of listening to these college professors over my car's sound system is that if my mind drifts for a few minutes, *I can simply rewind the tape or CD and listen to that section again.* In fact, if I mentally process something I have just heard for an extended length of time, I just hit the stop button until I am satisfied I have achieved some level of understanding, hitting the play button when I am ready to proceed. I may hear less of the tape over a given period of time, but I understand more *because I was able to take the time to process the information before proceeding with the lecture.*

In a classroom where a teacher or professor feels the need to "cover the material" quickly, this kind of immediate processing is not possible. A student who has to listen, take notes, and deal with external distractions (extraneous noises, an uncomfortable temperature, an annoying classmate)—all at the same time—can't simply stop and process something that interests her *because more notes have to be taken, and more material has to be covered before the class ends.* Good teachers hit the pause buttons on their own "teacher talk" in order to ask questions and give students a chance to process this new information while surfacing their own prior knowledge about the topic.

In addition to asking open-ended questions, it is important to allow students to discuss the information with other students in pairs, trios, or larger groups. Brooks and Brooks (1999) affirm, "Discourse with one's peer group is a critical factor in learning and development. Schools need to create settings that foster such interaction" (p. 111). Classrooms where teachers are doing all the talking are classrooms where teachers are doing all the work. Students know how to play the game in these cases; they can smile and go to a better place in their minds, nodding occasionally while taking a few notes. The teacher gets a *workout* while the kids seek a *way* out.

In the example that opened this chapter, Dana Hand's third-grade classroom, Hand takes every opportunity to harness her kid's energy, along with their natural tendency toward social discourse. Having shown a short video clip, for example, she wants them to process the information immediately after the clip ends. She is creative in her approach to the interaction of her third graders, and her kids appreciate the opportunity to move, along with the novelty connected with a "shower of words" that allow them to ham it up while reflecting on important points from the video. The music, the movement, the processing—all this is accentuated by kids who are whispering, speaking loudly or angrily, exaggerating, or acting surprised as they share with one another—makes for a wonderful combination that makes learning fun and interesting for Hand's students. Having visited her classroom, I can attest to the fact that Hand is constantly in search of new ways to make her classroom click, while making her own job interesting and rewarding.

One important key to success, then, is to shift students from passive observers to active participants. This, as I have observed over the years, is true of adults as well. It does not take long for any adult participant in a staff-development activity to infer that if the session facilitator has been reading from one PowerPoint slide after another, the rest of the two- or three-hour session is likely to go that way as well. What these adult participants tell me they do in this situation is to "go to a better place in their minds." One of my workshop participants once told me she drove two hours to get to my session, and during that drive she convinced herself she could "survive" four hours with me if she steeled herself to emerge at the end of that session awake and unscathed. Having been in my very interactive session for four hours, she reported that it was a pleasant surprise to find out she was not simply an observer in one more seemingly interminable "sit and git" class.

Students at every level, along with adults, appreciate the interactivity and effervescence of classrooms that are participant centered, rather than presenter centered. Having observed in hundreds of American classrooms over the course of my career, I can report with a great deal of certainty that students are happiest when they get to *do* something, *touch* something, *explain* something, *sing* something, *measure* something, *discuss* something, *question* something, *infer* something—and *learn* something in the process. Classrooms click when teachers shift the workload from themselves to their students. Put simply, being active in the pursuit of learning is a whole lot more fun and productive than watching the teacher or workshop facilitator work.

Keeping Them *All* Involved

Over the years, it has become apparent to me that many of our lesson plans live in a sort of fantasy world, and they plummet back to earth in the face of student passivity or ambivalence, a lack of sufficient time, unwarranted interruptions, or for any number of other reasons. A plan that looks great on paper may fall apart when, for example, a set of instructions given verbally seem not to have been understood. The plan may unravel when students who are not directly involved in a colloquy between the teacher and a few class favorites decide to mentally punch out for the duration of the activity. Whenever there are students who are not engaged, the best-laid plans can go astray.

I once observed an elementary classroom where one of the students was with the teacher at an interactive whiteboard, working on a short series of grammatical problems where the student's task was to identify what needed fixed and then fix it. Some of the students were looking at the board while others seemed to me to have gone to a better place in their minds. The student who had been at the board for maybe 2 minutes sat down, and his body language at that point said, "My work is done here." In short, for maybe 20 minutes, individual students were involved while at the board with the teacher, while those at their seats (*most* of the kids *most* of the time) were not engaged or connected in any meaningful way. When designing lessons, the trick is to figure out ways to involve all of the students most of the time.

In the examples from Elizabeth Scheine's kindergarten classroom (beginning on page 79), the teacher's role is that of facilitator of process as she checks for understanding during the activity. To do this, she need only observe how many students have selected the right answer. Over the course of several minutes, she can determine through their responses which students will need help with the phonemes concept or with end-of-sentence punctuation. Rather than have one student at the board while the others observe, *everyone is involved during the entire activity.*

Elizabeth Scheine—Kindergarten

In her kindergarten classroom, Elizabeth Scheine considered ways to involve her students in a unit on phonemes. She had an interactive whiteboard, but understood that only one student could be involved at any one time if the entire activity revolved around actually using the board. Combining modern interactive software with some old-fashioned sentence strips, Scheine hit upon a solution.

The student at the interactive board selected a picture and, with her finger, moved it into one of three boxes on the screen; each box was designated two phonemes (as in the word egg), three phonemes (cat), or four phonemes (flag). While the student at the board thought about where to put the picture, the children in the class were using their sentence strips to select the answer (two, three, or four). Each student had a clothespin, and he or she simply clipped the pin above the right number. The sentence strip in Figure 6.1 shows the proper placement of the pin for a word with four phonemes. The students showed Scheine what they thought the answer was, and the student at the board made her decision—with the result that everyone in the class was involved.

Figure 6.1 This is an example of what might be created, laminated, and given to the students, so everyone can be involved when one of their classmates is at the interactive whiteboard. In this example, the student has clipped the clothespin above the number 4 to represent four phonemes.

Created by Dianne Kinnison

(Continued)

(Continued)

Scheine subsequently used the same concept when practicing punctuation skills. As sentences appeared on the interactive whiteboard, students could decide whether they should end with question marks, periods, or exclamation marks. Once again, her kindergarteners used clothespins and a strip of paper with the three punctuation symbols, as in Figure 6.2 below.

Figure 6.2   In this case, the teacher reveals a sentence that requires the use of an exclamation point. The student clips the clothespin to the laminated strip in the proper place, showing it to the teacher.

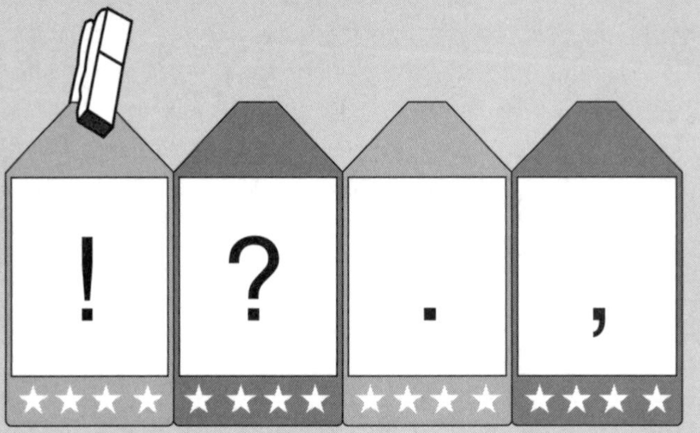

Created by Dianne Kinnison

None of the children in Scheine's class has the opportunity to opt out or simply wait passively for their turn at the interactive whiteboard. She engages them directly from the beginning.

By contrast, teachers who work with one student at the board (interactive or otherwise) may run themselves ragged, turning around constantly in order to remind the rest of the class to stay focused (or stay awake). Rather than fight this losing battle, teachers would do well to work into their plans strategies to involve everyone simultaneously. This shift from a mainly passive role to one that is far more active will benefit students and teachers alike. This takes some prior planning on the part of teachers, but the results are quite likely to make it well worth the effort. The "props" in Figures 6.1 and 6.2

can be laminated and used year after year. It is a low-tech solution with a high-impact reward.

Increasing Interaction While Lowering Tension Levels

Any teacher who wants to shift from a passive to a more interactive classroom is going to run into a roadblock created by the fear many students have of speaking in front of their classmates. In any list of the worst fears of humans, public speaking always comes at or near the top. I know teachers who can work with students all day long for an entire career; yet they hate getting in front of an adult audience. For some students, speaking to 30 of their peers in a classroom setting is uncomfortable at best and downright frightening at worst. One problem for a student can be the perceived or real reactions of his peers when he opens himself up in front of the class. He may be afraid of being wrong or misunderstood or making a misstep in the articulation of a point of view; he may be afraid of the quick and merciless judgments of his classmates in a classroom where the teacher allows such negative reactions to occur.

This potential obstacle is one that teachers are going to have to deal with in different ways. From the first minute of class on the first day of school, teachers need to make it clear that unsafe behavior is simply not tolerated. Students need to understand that neither the students *nor the teacher* will use scolding, sarcasm, or biting humor in the classroom. Teachers who want students to contribute verbally in the classroom will need to eliminate these negative behaviors from the beginning. Otherwise, even students who *might* contribute orally on occasion will cease doing so because of what others in the class might say or demonstrate through inappropriate body language. Students will immediately perceive such negative reactions on the part of classmates as threats, and this "triggers survival-oriented emotions and behaviors which get in the way of learning" (Bluestein, 2001, p. 31). It also gets in the way of communication.

When students share anything in class, whether it is the answer to a specific question, an opinion, or indeed any other information, teachers need to model a thoughtful and empathetic response. This means we need to develop our skills as listeners and teach those skills to our students. It means teaching students to actively practice the art of listening. According to Costa (2008), "We want our students to learn to devote their mental energies to another person and invest themselves in their partner's ideas" (p. 33). Costa continues, "We wish students to learn to hold in abeyance their own values, judgments, opinions, and prejudices in order to listen to and entertain another person's thoughts" (p. 33). In the classroom, teachers can accelerate this process *by modeling active listening at every turn.*

Teachers can also spend some time during the first week of school working with students on the development of active-listening skills. Reflecting on our own experiences informs us that body language can be negative or neutral; students who roll their eyes, yawn, shake their heads, frown, laugh derisively, fold their arms, or refuse to make eye contact with the speaker will short-circuit any conversation of which they are a part. Such behaviors communicate a great deal, and the combined weight of these neg-ative displays can easily—and tragically—keep a student who is speaking to her peers from wanting to do so ever again. If class-rooms are not emotionally safe places, students withdraw inwards and learning suffers.

Eye contact is another powerful listening skill, and students who spend a good deal of time staring at a computer screen may not find making eye contact either natural or comfortable. This means teach-ers need to spend a good deal of classroom time letting students practice having simple conversations with others while practicing good body language, appropriate facial expressions, and consistent eye contact. The first week of school is the perfect opportunity for teachers to turning these components of active listening into routine aspects of paired, small-group, and large-group discussions. Additionally, as Walsh and Sattes (2005) point out, once teachers ask a question of a student, they are called upon to "listen actively and attentively to student answers—and to be open to what each student is saying" (p. 108). One way to facilitate thinking on the part of students is to allow plenty of wait time (three to five seconds) after asking the question. According to Walsh and Sattes, increased wait time leads to an increase in the quality of the student answers. In the case of the number of answers from students, those can increase by 300% to 700% (pp. 80–81).

Teachers who do not choose to model effective listening should not be surprised when students with no training whatsoever in oral communication fail to listen actively, effectively, and productively. Human social interaction is a natural process; but, listening with empathy, avoiding judgments, making eye contact, affecting positive body language and facial expressions—all this must generally be learned. This is process, and teachers must teach it early in the year, *before the bad habits of a lifetime take root in the new classroom setting.* This requires teachers to be proactive, and it means the teaching of these oral communication skills must be part of the planning process during the summer.

Ramping Up Information Processing and Communication Skills

For students who may be reluctant to speak in front of the entire class, or even in a group of four or five classmates, the place to start is with paired discussions. In order to practice paired conversations, teachers can begin with a topic their students know well—themselves. Students can face a partner and practice both speaking and listening in a controlled setting, where students are talking to a partner who is practicing the art of listening. Topics for these early efforts might include describing a favorite meal, reviewing a favorite movie, or describing a fantastic vacation. I know teachers who have students hold fake microphones as they "interview" classmates on various topics. One advocate of these interviews is fifth-grade teacher Cindy Rickert, who marvels that students who are normally quiet and reserved become great interviewers as long as they have the microphone in their hands.

The idea here, of course, is that teachers can work up from pairs to trios to quartets on their way to getting students comfortable with the idea of sharing information, explaining something, or even defending a point of view. A teacher who has had his students taking part in regular, paired discussions over a few weeks can then debrief the whole process with the kids. Do they now feel comfortable having the paired discussions? Did the interactions get easier over the course of several days or weeks? Did they learn from each other in the course of content-related conversations? Is there anything that can be done in general to improve the process? One teacher of autistic children told me that while students felt uncomfortable talking to the entire class, they would have basic conversations with a partner.

Gary Spedden, a high-school teacher, has become proficient at facilitating movement and student-to-student processing in his history classroom. Having his students stand, find a partner, and take part in a pair-share activity "encourages positive interactions, reduces the fear of public embarrassment by not knowing an answer in front of the whole class, while allowing students to move, interact, and be the social creatures they are" (personal communication, November 6, 2009). Spedden understands that the teens in his class have to move, and they have to talk; instead of fighting that, he turns it to his—and their—advantage through the use of activities that encourage both movement and discussion.

The following review activity from Spedden's 12th-grade U.S. government class takes a total of about 25 to 30 minutes and is structured in two phases. During the first phase of the activity, students are standing and meeting with several partners in turn. The second part is devoted to students going over the answers obtained during the first phase, correcting what needs to be corrected and asking specific questions of Spedden only when all teams are finished.

Gary Spedden—Grade 12 U. S. Government

Before phase one begins, the students receive a review sheet with a series of questions that relate to the history and origins of our government. Some of the 20 review questions in this case include

In mercantilism, should imports or exports be greater? Why?

Give two names for the laws designed to punish colonists for the Boston Tea Party.

The purpose of the Philadelphia Convention was to _____ the Articles.

Explain salutary neglect.

Explain the 3/5 Compromise.

With handout in hand, each student meets with a classmate, asking that student if he knows the answer to one of the review questions. Once the partner finds a question he can answer, he answers out loud. If the student who did the asking agrees as to the answer (providing a correction if necessary), she writes it down on her own sheet. The student who provided the answer initials her sheet, and they both move on in search of other classmates as they move toward completing as much of the review sheet as possible. Spedden keeps track of time, gauging progress among his students, and calls a halt to the first phase of the activity when it is time.

On Spedden's cue, students return to their desks and to their regular teams of four. Beginning with Person 2, each team goes over the answers. If corrections need to be made on individual review sheets, that is done before moving on. Once the teams are finished, any unanswered questions are circled; only then does Spedden get involved in order to clear up any uncertainties or confusion. He also takes the time to debrief with his students as it relates to process. While content is the purpose of the activity, Spedden understands that the process bugs need to be eliminated on the way to continuous improvement. Lessons learned from this review will contribute to the smooth running of the next interactive exercise.

In my early days as a social studies teacher, I would have had students seated and quiet as they worked individually on a review sheet like this. Gary Spedden understands that having students move, collaborate, compare and defend answers, and otherwise become actively involved in their own learning is far more effective, interesting, and productive for students. During the entire activity, Spedden is able to take a balcony view of the proceedings; he circulates, listens, provides gentle reminders as to process, and works with students one on one. He makes plenty of mental notes relating to content and process alike, something that enables him to address whatever needs to be addressed when the activity has been completed.

What Makes Teachers Tick?

Finding the answer to this question reminds me of the chicken and the egg argument. Does a teacher who "ticks" result in a classroom that "clicks"? My sense is that teachers who are successful in establishing a safe environment and choreographing great instruction go a long way toward ensuring student progress and success. It is also true that the happiest teachers I have met over the years find their own forward progress accelerated by the high level of excitement, improvement, and appreciation shown by the students in their care. *Synergy* may be the operative word in highly successful classrooms where students and teachers contribute equally to the ultimate goal of performance improvement and skills development.

I'm also convinced that teachers thrive in building environments where they are demonstrably valued and supported. Where principals facilitate meaningful professional-development training and thus increase the instructional-delivery choices available to teachers, students and teachers benefit. When administrators effectively utilize formative feedback on the way to required—but often less-meaningful and timely—summative evaluations, teachers can make midcourse corrections and adjustments necessary to continuous improvement. When everyone in the building contributes to the success of new teachers, once again, everyone benefits.

Decisions made at the district and building level can have substantial impact on teachers—both negative and positive. No teacher alive would fight the reduction of paperwork in the schoolhouse. I have spoken to teachers whose principals have worked with vertical leadership teams in the building to do just that, saving trees, money, and—best of all from a teacher's point of view—time. Districts that devote one afternoon a month to professional development, often in the face of initial disapproval from parents, move their teachers and students down the continuous-improvement highway—provided, of course, that the professional development is thoughtfully and carefully designed for maximum impact.

Teachers want to be successful. Teachers want their students to taste success on a daily basis; this means the building-level focus needs to be on instruction. Leadership teams in effective schools work steadily and relentlessly along a continuous-improvement highway that has parents sending their kids there every day *confident in the instructional outcomes.* Building administrators and teachers in effective schools understand that nothing changes until something changes. In the best schools, teachers try things, evaluate, adjust, and move inexorably forward. There is no school, teacher, or student who cannot improve on the way things are right now; principals who keep their instructional focus are, in my experience, more likely to succeed.

Fullan (2010) puts this most succinctly: "To get anywhere, you have to *do* something" (p. 32). In schools that move relentlessly forward, the bias is toward trying things, doing things, and then reflecting on how it went—all in anticipation of taking the next step forward. This takes leadership on the part of administrators—who are also learners. Highly successful instructional leaders talk with teachers, walk with teachers, take risks with teachers, and they learn with teachers. "Leaders must learn to become change savvy by reflective doing. . . . It works because the group develops capacity and begins to believe in themselves because they see the results" (Fullan, 2010, p. 33). When human beings begin to see that something they did resulted in forward movement, they build collective confidence in their capacity to do that again and again and again.

Kathy Hwang—Principal

Sanders Corner Elementary School is located in Loudoun County, a rapidly expanding northern Virginia school district. Sanders Corner's principal, Kathy Hwang, has been at the school for several years; her focus on instruction is laser sharp, with the result that a school that has always been good continues to get better. Hwang and her leadership team, motivated by a belief that students need to be engaged in their own learning, sought a way to embed professional development into the instructional fabric of Sanders Corner. Teachers were provided with copies of my book The Active Classroom *(2008), in the spring of 2008, with the understanding they would read it over the summer. When the teachers returned in August, they were divided into study groups; each group collaboratively processed a single chapter in jigsaw fashion, reporting back to the entire faculty in turn during inservice sessions.*

During those sessions, teams provided their peers with ideas as to how what they called the active engagement (AE) strategies might be used at the various grade levels. Hwang visits classrooms often, and during that 2008–2009 school year, pre- and post-observation conferences included reflections on where and how AE strategies were being employed with students. In March 2009, Hwang sent a team of 16 teachers to a one-day conference where they picked up more strategies, along with copies of Green Light Classrooms *(2008), by Dr. Rich Allen. At the last staff meeting in the spring, teachers paired up and conducted a "walk and talk," the purpose of which was to allow teachers to reflect on these four questions:*

1. *Where am I with active engagement in the classroom?*

2. *What will I commit to trying in 2009–2010?*

3. *What assistance do I anticipate I will need?*

4. *What did I learn from my walking partner during the "walk and talk" activity?*

At the end of this last staff session, teachers wrote their answers to these four questions on an exit ticket; the feedback thus gained helped guide Hwang and her leadership team as they prepared for a new school year— and another opportunity to examine how they do what they do in an innovative and truly reflective school and classroom environment.

After many visits to Sanders Corner, I can conclude with certainty that this school community's progress on the continuous-improvement highway is both steady and relentless. Teachers know exactly what to expect—and the expectations are both predictably high and fully attainable. Success at Sanders Corner comes by way of a collaborative effort that generates excitement through innovation, experimentation, and a willingness to take risks on behalf of kids.

Final Thoughts

Some years ago, I ran across a quote to the effect that teachers live for the moment when the kids "get it." I believe this, and I think teachers tick and classrooms click when Eddie lights up with the realization he just did something today he could not do yesterday. This is true of teachers as well; I have seen the faces and received the e-mails from teachers who took a risk *and tried something new that worked.*

In Chapter 7, we'll look at the uses of humor, storytelling, novelty, and other things that will energize students and teachers alike.

7

Think Pair Share

Energize, Energize, Energize

I remember a history teacher who told terrible jokes. He knew they were ter-rible jokes; we knew they were terrible jokes; he knew we knew they were terrible jokes . . . and we laughed anyway. We looked forward to them, and we looked forward to his class. A few years later, I had a college professor who told wonderful stories, laced with humor and irony; we loved hearing them. A good friend of mine was teacher of the year at his high school for several years in a row. His sense of humor is second to none, and I have no doubt his students looked forward to walking into his classroom. All three of these teachers had the ability to make people laugh, and laughter is indeed good medicine, both figuratively and literally. Appropriate laughter energizes, and it makes students want to come back for more.

I have always found appropriate laughter to be wonderfully thera-peutic. It lightens a mood; and in a classroom, it provides a needed change of mental state for students who have been sitting and taking notes for some time. Garmston (1997) points out that laughter "clears the mind, refreshing the screen on each individual's personal computer" (p. 77). There may be nothing so engaging, and ultimately satisfying, as a good story replete with humor; my guess is that any person who can remember his or her favorite teacher may well count among that teacher's qualities a great sense of humor. This salient fact should not be lost on today's teachers and administrators.

As affirmed by Smith (2005), it turns out that laughter not only affects our state of mind, it also positively affects our immune systems, lowers blood pressure, and relieves stress (p. 162). Many teachers I know have their students sing at the drop of a hat, and the songs they sing are often silly and therefore funny. Humor is a powerful tool for teachers, and my experience is that little gets the attention of students as quickly or as completely. Sousa (2001) reminds us, "emotions enhance retention, so the positive feelings that result from laughter increase the probability that students will remember what they learned" (p. 63).

Kaufeldt (2005) qualifies this correctly by saying, "As long as the humor isn't sarcastic or a joke at someone else's expense, opportunities to laugh should be included in every lesson" (p. 56). The use of inappropriate humor can create an unsafe classroom where no student is quite sure who the next target might be. Teachers should not only avoid their own use of sarcasm, they should also make certain students do not use it during class. Nothing will sour classroom climate as much as inappropriate humor.

Self-deprecating humor is appropriate and effective. It shows teachers to be human, and it demonstrates that the teacher who uses it can laugh at his or her own imperfections or actions. When working with teachers and administrators around the country, I share the delicious irony of my *spending a good deal of time* in the faculty lounge early in my career *complaining about a lack of time*. I also joke about my propensity, again during my early years in the profession, to lecture frequently using an overhead projector in a darkened room, something my former students may not remember as particularly humorous . . . or enlightening. Come to think of it, they may not remember it at all if they went to a better place in their minds while I droned on about this war or that Supreme Court case. In this way, and with these stories, I get my point across without seeming to preach.

Four decades of observing teachers has taught me that those teachers who are naturally funny, or those teachers who take the time to incorporate humor into their lessons, are not only more successful in the classroom but are also happier campers. I have observed teachers whose classrooms are pretty dour places because humor is not part of their repertoire. Teachers who think there is no place for humor in the classroom may be in for a bumpy ride with kids who appreciate a sense of humor. Laughter releases endorphins that make students feel good, even as it releases more oxygen into the bloodstream (Sousa, 2001, p. 63). Humor is cheap, dependable, and effective. To be effective, however, it must be utilized—and that requires planning.

A key consideration, of course, is that many teachers realize they simply are not funny people. Those who feel they are in that category may feel they can't add humor to the mix because it does not come naturally. The good news is that there are several ways to infuse humor into the classroom, and thoughtful preparation can make it so.

Energizing With Stories

In the process of writing this book one fall morning, I found myself in a bit of a depressed mood. I had not slept well the night before, and the sun had not broken through the clouds in the course of many rainy days. In short, I was in need of an energy boost. While running some errands, I stopped by the local library and picked up a book on tape narrated by Bill Wallis. Wallis is a wonderful storyteller, and never more at his best than when narrating a book in the *Rumpole of the Bailey* series, by John Mortimer. Mortimer's fictional character, Horace Rumpole, is an irascible, highly intelligent, small-cigar-smoking British barrister who also happens to be incredibly funny; and Bill Wallis brings Rumpole to life with his narration. I popped the tape into my car stereo as soon as I left the library, and within a short time I was smiling—and then laughing out loud. The somber mood of a few minutes before had been replaced by a feeling of euphoria; the bad weather and lack of sleep had been trumped by a great story, written by a great storyteller, and told by a great narrator.

Harnessing the power of storytelling is something every teacher can do in the classroom and something every administrator can do when teachers and staff are gathered together for any purpose. Funny stories, as long as they are not told at the expense of another person, can set just the right tone for a classroom lesson or a faculty meeting. As I was able to do with myself on that day when I found myself a bit down in the dumps, humor-laced stories can serve as powerful medicine. Beginning with a humorous story serves to get everyone's attention and get lessons or meetings off to a fast start.

In his book *The Power of Personal Storytelling*, Jack McGuire (1998) says that personal stories "may or may not include outright chortles, giggles, or guffaws" (p. 25). His definition of humor is "our ability to delight, smile, and laugh at the wonder of life, as a child does" (p. 25). My experience is that when teachers shift from third person (in social studies, for example) to first person, students pay attention. Any teacher who pauses, looks at the kids, and says, "You won't believe what happened to me over the weekend!" immediately has the attention of every student in the room. A story about a car that would not start on a cold winter day might serve as the perfect doorway into a discussion of the Continental Army's difficult winter at Valley Forge during the Revolutionary War. Such personal stories can be both interesting and useful in the classroom.

Stories replete with humor, personal or otherwise, connect with students. Stories also serve as a tool teachers can use to get students to focus on a particular issue or content-related subject. Anyone dealing with modern British history must deal with perhaps the greatest British historical figure of the modern era—Winston Churchill. The doorway into Churchill's life might be opened for students of any age by pointing out how much trouble he had with math. He always said he could not understand why numbers were always in debt to one another . . . borrowing from each other and then having to pay back the "loan." This small facet of Churchill's life may resonate loudly with any student whose favorite subject is *not* mathematics. The clear implication here is that great leaders—or the rest of us, for that matter—need not be proficient in everything. Whatever weaknesses Churchill possessed did not preclude him from making his indelible mark on the history of Britain and the world. It is the area where our strengths lie that will most likely determine our ultimate success in the world of work. Social studies teachers work in an area replete with countless personal stories that will ring a bell with students of any generation and open the door to any number of content-related issues.

The *how* of storytelling is at least as important as the *what*. Teachers and administrators need to reflect on what makes a good story powerful as well as on what makes what *could* have been a good story ineffective. There really are some things teachers can work on that will add impact to the stories they tell.

1. *Consider your audience.* By this, I mean run through your story and look for distracters. For example, if you use vocabulary with which members of your audience are not likely to be familiar, many of them will be distracted as they try to figure out what a particular word, phrase, or reference is all about. For them, the thread of your story is lost as they temporarily disengage in order to make sense of something. If you need to explain something in advance, do that *before you begin to tell the story.*

2. *Change the physical state of your students.* If students have been sitting in their desks for some time, get them to move to somewhere else in the room. For elementary students, this may mean moving them to a rug that is placed in a corner or in the center of the room. I know middle-school teachers who will

clear away the front row of desks and have students sit on the floor in front of the teacher. For high-school students, it may mean having them stand, get a handout from a few stacks around the room, and then return to their desks; this gives them a break before you begin to tell the story.

3. *Minimize distractions in the room.* Visual always trumps auditory; if you have something on the screen, turn it off before you begin. If you have a remote for a PowerPoint slide, black out the slide until you are done; otherwise, the image will serve as a distraction. Close the door to the hall if noise out there is likely to distract students.

4. *Silence is golden . . . and effective as an attention getter.* Before you begin, look away for a few seconds, and then look back at your audience. This silence builds interest and anticipation far better than anything you are likely to vocalize. Don't tell them you are going to tell them a story . . . just tell it.

5. *Your own distractions are, well, distracting.* Keep your gestures to a minimum, unless the gestures will contribute to the story. When describing a "teeny little bug," for instance, putting your thumb and forefinger together, tilting your head, and closing one eye can help emphasize or highlight the image. However, a storyteller who throws his arms around constantly may distract listeners. Remember, visual always trumps auditory, as evidenced by the way Internet Web sites try to get your attention. Try as we might when we are online, it is hard to ignore a dancing person, a bouncing ball, or a car that is rotating in a small picture frame. (Our brains like novelty, and companies advertising on the Internet know and rely on that.)

6. *Work to identify and eliminate verbal distractions.* We have all, I would guess, fixated on nonwords some speakers use . . . *um* is a typical example. I can remember a presentation where I, as an audience member, realized the speaker was using *um* frequently. I must admit I started counting the number of times I heard it, something that made it impossible for me to listen closely and focus on the topic at hand. Early in my career as a presenter, I had a friend of mine in my audience—someone who had seen me present on that particular topic before—count the number of times I said *um* for a full half hour. He reported I used that distracting nonword 17 times. That surprised me, and it helped me eliminate that unfortunate distraction in favor of silence.

7. *If possible, practice your story in advance.* As you practice, think about inflection, volume, timing, and pitch. Lowering your voice during the story is powerful, and your students' brains will attend to this change in volume. Think about places you can stop briefly, giving your students a chance to process and predict.

8. *In your car on the way to work, listen to books on tape or CD.* Most of those who narrate audio books are professionals, and you can learn much from them. If your stories have characters, listening to professional narrators can give you ideas of how to adjust your voice for various characters in your own stories.

9. *Set aside a location in the room to which you can go when it is time to tell a story.* Some teachers will have stools or captains' chairs in some permanent location in the room and will simply go there when it is story time. I have known teachers who encourage *students* to tell stories from that location as well.

A good way to see how effective you are as a storyteller is to have someone record you, so you can see yourself as others see—and hear—you. This gives you an opportunity to listen to yourself without attending to how you look; it provides you with a chance to turn the volume off in order to check out your gestures, body language, and facial expressions. You will notice those things—visual and auditory—that distract from the story.

The Role of Emotion

Sprenger (2005) affirms, "because emotions are so powerful, incorporating emotion into our teaching is an excellent way to reach our students" (p. 23). Stories frequently contain emotion all along a continuum from gut-busting laughter on one end to tears at the other. Emotion enhances memory, and Sprenger reminds us, "we remember poignant events better than boring or neutral ones" (p. 22). I can remember exactly where I was, what I was doing, and what the room looked like the day we heard in school that John Kennedy had been assassinated. I can remember exactly where I sat, where the wall-mounted speaker was located, and where the teacher was sitting as he put his head in his hands and cried. By the same token, I can remember with great clarity where I was, who I was with, and what the living room looked like in February 1964, when the Beatles appeared on the *Ed Sullivan Show* on that Sunday evening. These events still bring back feelings on both ends of the emotional spectrum, and I have no doubt the memories associated with those two events will not easily fade with time—and they took place over 45 years ago.

Teachers, especially those who rely on lecture, may want to explore the uses of storytelling in providing a different approach to understanding and memory. Great teachers make teaching and learning memorable, and stories are a unique and effective way of imparting information, getting the attention of students, and enhancing their memories.

Energizing With Music

One of the most effective mood enhancers I have encountered in classrooms is music. Upbeat music creates an upbeat mood, and kids who are in school for seven hours need that kind of stimulation. In every case where I have observed music being used to transition from one activity to another, it has been accompanied by smiles and laughter. In one elementary classroom, I watched—and laughed—when a first grader, on hearing the opening bars of "Get Ready" by The Temptations (the teacher's transition song), jumped to her feet and said, "Wow!" She then moved quickly to the station the teacher had assigned to her, and she continued to sort of "groove in place" until all her classmates were where they should be and the music stopped.

Nikki Martel—Third-Grade Teacher

In Martel's third-grade classroom, students transition from their seats into pairs or small groups to the accompaniment of upbeat songs like "We Got the Beat" (GoGos). Rather than tell students it is time to clean up, Martel simply plays Roy Orbison's "Pretty Woman," and they clean up their workspaces before moving to another activity. A different song is used to line students up before they leave the classroom to go to the gym, cafeteria, or another classroom. Again, there is no need for a verbal cue from Martel—the music does the work for her.

Martel often has her students stand and meet with a partner in order to have content-related conversations. I observed this in her classroom one morning, and I can report that once the students had grooved their way to their new locations, they were ready to discuss the topic at hand with their partners. Martel understands the important role of music as a process facilitator. The use of movement and music is a powerful combination, and Martel's elementary students approach learning in a much more receptive frame of mind when music is part of the transition mix. In middle- and high-school classrooms where teachers play music as the students enter or leave the room, the mood is lifted. One teacher once told me she eliminated tardies by playing music as students came into the room at the beginning of class. Another teacher, on Fridays, plays "Na Na, Hey Hey, Goodbye" by Steam as the students exit the room. A Texas elementary-school librarian plays "We Are the Dinosaurs (Marching, Marching!)" as the kids march out of the library after a session with her. The students love it, and the use of music is both cheap and effective. Having observed hundreds of classrooms, I can truly say that where music is present, the general atmosphere is lighter, and the energy level is high.

The repeated use of humor, music, and movement by teachers provides students with an outlet for their energy as well as a valuable change of state. Over the years, I have observed that in classrooms where students have plenty of opportunities to stand, move, talk, share . . . and laugh, teachers have fewer management problems than those who try to "keep the lid" on things by having students sit quietly and do individual seatwork all day or all period long.

Teachers can frequently get students to stand and do some simple exercises as part of a transition from one classroom activity to another. Educators also need to make sure kids get plenty of exercise during recess as well as in regularly scheduled physical-education classes. Conversations with parents need not just be about grades; teachers and administrators can encourage parents to make certain that their kids get plenty of exercise at home. This is critical in an age when sitting in front of a screen has increasingly replaced the outdoor activities that were commonplace during the childhood of previous generations. Every bit of movement and exercise helps, but nothing will replace an all-out effort to raise the fitness level of young people. Medina (2008) tells us, "Brain-activation studies show that children and adolescents who are fit allocate more cognitive resources to a task and do so for longer periods of time" (p. 18). If exercise and movement raises the energy level of students and assists with cognition, then we all need to commit to providing as much of it as possible.

Energizing Staff

I can't speak for anyone else in education today, but I can relate that I did not always look forward to going to faculty meetings. They were, all too often, information dumps whose purpose might have been served by distributing a timely memo. Too often in these meetings, there was normally little give and take; the object was often to get it over with, so we could get on with whatever else we were doing. There were, as I recall, few attempts to infuse humor, music, movement, or reflection into the mix. We sat, we listened, and we left.

Here are some suggestions for principals who want to pump energy into one- or two-hour meetings with faculty and staff:

1. *Have some upbeat music playing when everyone is entering the meeting location.* I received an e-mail from a central-office instructional coordinator who told me that having music playing when the teachers with whom she is working enter the room lifts their individual and collective mood; its repeated use during the workshop makes it much easier to teach and reach them. Make sure you include (appropriate!) music from several decades, popular tunes from the 60s, 70s, 80s, 90s, and today. When you hit someone's favorite song or musical group, you will know it (and they will appreciate it).

2. *Keep the one-sided flow of information to a minimum.* If you use electronic slides, keep the font size large (22 point or above), and *don't read to your staff what they can read for themselves.* Turn off the slide when you want to talk with your faculty. (Make certain you are not between the projector and the screen; otherwise, the image may be projected on your good self. This is a powerful—and preventable—visual distracter.)

3. *Get your participants involved in activities that are meaningful and purposeful.* If you are hearing from several sources about a problem that exists in the school, bring it up and put them in groups to begin to sort it out. In so doing, they can answer key questions like, *What is the root problem?* and, *What steps might we take to solve it?* My experience is that teachers and staff who are closest to the problems in the building are also closest to the solutions; those that are involved in solving the problems may be more invested in the *implementation* of those solutions. Knowing everyone has worked together to solve something in the school is energizing in itself.

4. *If teachers and staff are working on problem solving in the meeting, make it clear as to what their role is in the process.* If they are empowered to make decisions in order to solve problems, let them know that. If the decision will be made by the administrators in

the building with *input* from teachers and staff, make that clear. Those at the meeting will be predictably unhappy (and de-energized) *if they thought they were making a decision about a solution for which they were really only providing input.* Clarity of communication is a critical role of leadership, and no more so than at meetings where staff members are involved in the continuous-improvement process.

5. *Every 10 minutes or so, get everyone standing, moving, and sharing with one another.* Once again, music—that universal energizer—can be used to transition them from their seats to their standing pairs or groups. To get their attention, simply bring the volume of the music up, and cut it off. (You'll need a remote for this.) I have done this for years in working with adults, and it works well. If you find people are singing along and swaying to the music, *let it happen!* If you are so inclined, sway and sing with them. I often bring the volume of the music up and then cut it off at an appropriate point, pulling my forefinger across my throat so that we all stop together, but not before we have all had some fun. This is particularly important if the meeting is at the end of a long day of school!

6. *Teachers love free stuff.* Gather together some door prizes to give away during the meeting, and take some time to acknowledge those who have accomplished something outstanding in the classroom, schoolhouse, or community. My suggestion is to *check with those people in advance to find out if they mind public recognition.* It may mean more to them for you as an administrator to compliment them privately than for you to make it public. I had a supervisor who asked us soon after she was hired, via e-mail, whether we preferred our praise public or private. She then held to that and honored those preferences.

7. *Start on time, and end on time.* Meet and greet staff members as they enter. If there are technical glitches that need to be solved, this should be taken care of by the time people start arriving. Greeting staff members communicates that they are important. You honor those who are on time by starting the event at the scheduled time. If more time is needed to work on a particular problem or issue, provide another opportunity for the group to meet or for a small-leadership cadre to meet and then report back to the staff. Extensive planning on the agenda, with activities that are timed—and where the timing is adhered to—should help make certain the meeting ends at the time indicated.

When the meeting is over, play more upbeat music as everyone leaves the room.

8. *Finally, follow up with staff members* on the disposition of everything that was proposed, discussed, and decided at the meeting. Teachers like to know that what they deliberated and decided meant something; they like to see the fruits of their labor in actions taken soon after the meeting. There is little that de-energizes staff members as much as realizing there will be no real follow-up to the meeting or that changes agreed upon will not be implemented. A faculty and staff who labor to produce something that is never put into place will be far less likely to want to return for another meeting, which, so far as they can see, will once again lead to nothing in the way of improvement or progress.

By making a commitment to energize meetings through the use of movement, music, collaborative activities, acknowledgement, appropriate praise, and principles of time management, administrators can model what teachers could and should be doing in the classroom. Administrators who basically lecture their way through a 45-minute meeting are modeling the kind of passive role for participants they may not want to see teachers utilizing in the classroom. Making faculty meetings truly productive, collaborative, and interesting will go a long way toward creating a school climate that is infused with positive energy and a commitment to continuous improvement.

Another way to ramp up success and energize teachers is to conduct book clubs within the building, involving books and articles based on everything from classroom management to brain-based learning. The reflective conversations that result from such professional-development activities can inform decision making for individual teachers or whole grade levels. If the conversations take place across grade levels, decisions can be made that affect vertical planning as well. Administrators can also assign small teams of staff members to each chapter of a book, instructing them to report out to the entire staff in a giant jigsaw activity that turns faculty meetings into *true* and *productive* faculty meetings where continuous improvement is the goal.

The Biggest Energizer of All

I believe one of the best ways to get teachers energized is to give them access to tons of strategies that will engage students in their own learning. This can be accomplished by providing opportunities for teachers to observe in other classrooms—inside their buildings or in other schools and districts. Many years ago, when I was an organizational-development specialist with the Virginia Beach Public Schools, a large group of about a dozen teachers, principals, and central-office administrators visited a North Carolina district that had done great things in the area of continuous improvement in general and student achievement in particular. Our drive home in two separate school vans, about 3 hours or so, was one of the most energizing and productive experiences of my four decades in the field of education.

That two-day visit resulted in a reciprocal visit to Virginia Beach by the principal, assistant principal, and several outstanding teachers from one elementary school. They made a presentation to over a hundred of our teachers and administrators that we were able to tape and use for many years. Our school district benefited immensely from this out-of-district visit, and I encourage district and building administrators to seek out the very best classrooms, within easy driving distance, and arrange reciprocal visits between and among schools. Classroom observations followed by a reflective conversation are powerful process-improvement tools.

One of the things I observed during that process is that the teachers and administrators from the school district we visited were extremely proud of what they had accomplished. Importantly, they were willing to share with us what they had done and learned over many years. The energy level of those professionals—teachers and administrators alike—was high, and this was because they were succeeding in reaching, teaching, and engaging their students. The students in the classrooms we visited loved every minute of what they were doing, in large measure because they were the ones doing the work. One eighth-grade class was involved in a problem-based learning activity directly related to a set of improvements in their school district. The teachers involved in that project facilitated process while the kids did the work. *They loved what they were accomplishing, and their energy level was off the chart.*

Final Thoughts

I have observed classrooms with little energy, and I have been in classrooms where the amount of energy produced could light a small city. Students who are watching video after video, listening to lecture after lecture, and completing worksheet after worksheet—all of this from their desks—are not likely to be either engaged or energized, especially in the 21st century. Education is not a spectator sport. Students at every level need to get up, move, pair, share, laugh, think . . . and learn. Show me a classroom with a teacher who understands this, and I will show you an environment conducive to learning.

By the same token, show me a school where the administrators understand this, and I will show you a school where teachers meet with other teachers, sharing what works and what doesn't. Show me a school with a well-stocked professional-development library with subscriptions to leading educational journals, along with a leadership team that guarantees its use in pursuit of excellence, and I will show you a faculty dedicated to continuous improvement. Show me a classroom environment that is learner centered, with a teacher who is just one more learner, and I will show you a bunch of kids who can't wait to get to school—and who can't wait to get home to tell their parents "what happened in school today."

In Chapter 8, we'll explore the power of professional reflection as a way to improve in the areas of instruction and leadership. Building a reflective capacity into the fabric of the school community ensures that even if the principal retires or transfers to another school, momentum is not lost, and the journey along the continuous-improvement highway does not slow or come to a halt.

8

Reflecting
on Reflection

When my parents divorced in the early 1950s, my father and I went to live with my grandparents in their house on Gibson Street in North East, Pennsylvania. There was a small chair in the corner of the dining room that saw a good deal of action, especially after a morning of building snow forts on a cold winter's day. I would come inside to find my grandmother had placed the chair in front of the register that brought heat up from the coal-fired furnace in the basement. She would bring me a cup of hot cider or cocoa, and I would remove my winter coat and dry out while sitting on the chair over the register.

The chair had another and more sinister use, from my vantage point as a six- or seven-year-old kid who knew how to get in trouble on occasion. When I got out of line, my grandfather would send me to that same chair and instruct me to think about what I had done. In this way, and on that small chair, I learned the power of reflection.

Reflection is a powerful tool for learning and for improvement. Garmston and Wellman (1999) underscore the need for collaborative groups working in schools to take the time to reflect on process: "Any group that is too busy to reflect on its work is too busy to improve" (p. 60). This is true of individual teachers as well. Teachers who consistently take the time to reflect on *how* they do *what* they do, even as they seek out *new* ways of connecting with and engaging students, all but guarantee forward progress. A great teacher is never really satisfied with the status quo, *and this attitude is not lost on the students in her care.* Kids are nothing if not perceptive, and they can spot a good teacher or a slacker a mile off. They enter a new classroom and observe carefully for a few days. Next, in constructivist fashion, they combine what they have learned about this new teacher with their knowledge base concerning *former* teachers; and they come to some conclusions about what life in this new classroom will be like. Their own personal inferences combine with those of their friends at lunchtime, and out of those between-bite conversations is forged a consensus view about life in Room 104.

Reflection is indeed our teacher, and we can learn much by taking the time to put our actions and lessons under a microscope. Moreover, we can enlist the help of other teachers by inviting them to come into our classrooms and observe with a purpose. By this, I mean teachers can ask a colleague to spend 20 to 30 minutes sitting at the back of the room and focusing on certain things. For example, the observing teacher might be asked to answer some process-related questions: Having asked a question of her students, does the classroom teacher allow three to five seconds of wait time before calling on someone? Does the classroom teacher use verbal distracters ("um" or "ah") while speaking? Does the body language of students (including facial expressions) indicate they are engaged? These are simple questions about important issues related to process, and these or other questions can form the basis for a reflective conversation between the two teachers at a time convenient for both to meet (without distractions).

Over the course of weeks or months, teachers at any grade level get *plenty* of experience. In order to improve, however, at some point they will need to hit the pause button and reflect on what is working and what is not. If I could get teachers all over the country to do one thing, it would be to continually examine their own processes in an effort to continually improve performance. If the reflection, alone or with colleagues, is not purposeful, then improvement will be impossible at worst or haphazard at best. Experience *plus* reflection *plus* action equals improved performance.

Teachers can also tap into the reflective capacities of students. As we indicated above, students possess a great deal of knowledge about what is effective or not when it comes to pedagogy. A teacher willing to spend 15 or 20 minutes per week working with students on what is and is not working from their standpoint—a pretty important standpoint—can get some valuable feedback that can be factored into that teacher's own reflective efforts in order to improve instruction. The key here is to understand that feedback is just feedback, and teachers can explain to students that *their input* as it relates to specific questions (Are you being engaged in this class? Do you feel it is safe to share and discuss things here?) is valuable as a catalyst for continuous improvement. I did this for my last two years of teaching, but I made the mistake of asking for feedback at the end of the year—great for next year's students, but useless for the kids with whom I had just spent the better part of nine months. Even if teachers did this once per month, beginning in early October, it would go a long way toward facilitating progress *and making students feel valued and empowered.*

Reflective Thinking

When I was in seventh grade, I had a music-appreciation teacher who insisted we listen to classical music. At the time, of course, we were teenagers and in love with the likes of Elvis, Fats Domino, Paul Anka, and everyone else on the Billboard charts. The last thing we wanted to listen to was classical music. We once scored a great victory, as I recall, by getting him to play "The Twist," by Chubby Checker, in the classroom. The bargain was that if he played "our" music, we would listen to "his" music. We grumbled, rolled our eyes, and protested; he played it anyway. I can remember how he closed his eyes and listened to one of Mozart's piano concertos. Under protest, we all sat and listened as well.

I fought it then, but I love it now; on my iPod, I have a playlist of nothing but classical compositions from Beethoven to Mozart to Vivaldi. A few years ago, I directed a large regional educational conference; by the time it was over on Saturday, I was exhausted. On Sunday, I attended a matinee performance of Mahler's Fifth Symphony, conducted by JoAnn Falletta, director of the Virginia Symphony Orchestra. I sat right down front, and I let the music wash over me while I reflected on the two-day conference just completed the previous day. I was able to listen to one of my favorite classical pieces, and I managed to run through the entire two days in my mind. Listening to classical music allows me to relax, reflect, and sort through complicated issues or problems. I thank my music teacher for sticking to his guns on the issue of what we were exposed to in that class.

On Friday evening of my two-day conference, I was able to reflect on the day's events, and I put in place changes on Saturday that, I believe, made things run more smoothly. Improvement-minded principals and building-level leadership teams do what they do, and then they make adjustments in the name of progress. Reflection is the name of the game in the improvement business. Schools are all about the improvement business; *indeed, it is their business.* The direction of a symphony, the direction of a conference, and the direction of an instructional program in the schoolhouse all have much in common. In each case, the trick is to pull together seemingly disparate elements into one harmonious whole. The symphony orchestra rehearses over and over again, making adjustments in the name of continuous improvement. Collaboratively, they stop, go over what they just rehearsed, and incorporate adjustments that make the performance better. Reflection is a powerful tool, if it is seen as such and used by teachers and administrators alike.

Working collaboratively, as we saw in Chapter 6 with Sanders Corner Elementary, effective schools reflect on where they are now, seek ways to improve, and subsequently make the necessary adjustments in order to move forward. At Sanders Corner they try this; they reject that; they keep what works; then, they celebrate and start the process all over. Progress is about process, and individual and collaborative reflection is a key and indispensable component to making something better. Knight (2007) reminds us that this is a fluid process, and "reflective thinkers, by definition, have to be free to choose or reject ideas, or else they are not thinkers at all" (p. 47). For individuals, reflection may come in quiet moments; for teachers and administrators working in collaborative groups, reflection may be an "out loud" exercise that benefits from multiple perspectives, different angles, and competing points of view.

Seeking and Accepting Feedback

One of my heroes is Dale Crownover, whose company, Texas Nameplate, won the prestigious Malcolm Baldrige National Quality Award in 1998 and again in 2004. While in Dallas many years ago, I arranged to visit this amazing company, and was given the tour by Dale Crownover himself. Over lunch that day, he impressed on me the importance of customer feedback in the continuous-improvement process. In his book *Take It to the Next Level*, Crownover (1999) recommends that leaders in any organization must "seek feedback and learn how to accept constructive criticism and even, sometimes, harsh criticism. It's very difficult to improve processes if you can't accept feedback" (p. 166). Leadership teams at the school and district level would do well to solicit feedback from teachers, parents, students, and graduates. Ten years down the road, for example, high-school graduates are in a good position to answer questions related to how well prepared they were for whatever it is they ended up doing in college and the workplace.

One of my favorite days during my tenure as a specialist in charge of our new-teacher orientation was the day I sat down to read the evaluations of that orientation week from hundreds of novice teachers as well as those veterans who were new to the district. Those of us who worked on this important weeklong induction program understood that we could substantially improve process if we sought out, and then carefully considered, feedback from those who attended the orientation. We made our own observations, of course, but the perspectives of four or five hundred teachers spoke volumes, and those comments proved to be valuable data that resulted in myriad improvements from year to year.

As teachers seek to shift their students from passive observers to active participants in their own learning, so administrators can shift their faculty and staff from passive recipients of top-down decisions to active participants in their own improvement cycles. I have always believed that those closest to the problems in an organization *are closest to the solutions.* Administrators who regularly enlist staff in the school's journey to excellence by trying to determine how things are going from their perspective will build trust and build the capacity for improvement from the bottom up. Seeking feedback at the building and district level shows those providing it that their opinions are respected.

Of one thing I am certain: feedback will surface, regardless of whether or not it was sought or encouraged by the building administrators. It will surface in the parking lot, the faculty lounge, and at the water fountains—but it will surface. It is the nature of human beings to offer opinions and make judgments, and I can remember clearly why I used to avoid the faculty lounge when possible. Everyone there has the solutions to problems that exist in the building. With no official outlet for their input, teachers often engage in rudderless conversations, the very existence of which often highlight a lack of any sort of systemic approach to improvement. It is far better to channel those opinions and that feedback into constructive conversations that result in positive change.

Actively Involving Everyone

Teachers do appreciate being heard, but positive results must be forthcoming from efforts to seek feedback. Simply soliciting feedback from teachers is not enough, and many teachers can perhaps point to surveys taken but never acted upon. Some surveys are launched with great fanfare—never to be mentioned again. If feedback is sought but never used to affect change, teachers will grow understandably cynical; they will be much less likely to cooperate the next time their feedback is sought. On the other hand, if faculty and staff members see that their collective feedback results in changes for the better, they will be more likely to participate in continuous-improvement efforts down the road.

My experience is that when faculty meetings shift from "administrivia" to a true instructional focus, with the active involvement of teachers in a truly reflective professional-development session, their energy levels rise, and much can be accomplished. Lezotte (1992) reminds us that students who are excited about school are those who are actively involved in their own learning, "rather than passive onlookers of the teacher" (p. 61). The same can be said of teachers; they are much more excited about school when they are actively involved in the building's continuous-improvement efforts rather than passive recipients of instructions or decrees from the office or district.

Active and Passive Classrooms

We are left with the salient fact that most students—and adults, from my experience—would rather be active than passive when it comes to what goes on in classrooms or workshops. Classrooms where students are mentally and physically engaged in process and content have a different look and feel about them. Anyone who spends even an hour in the active classroom observing students and teachers alike will see and hear something along the lines of Figure 8.1. Arrangements should be made for new teachers to visit classrooms like this—and then reflect on the experience individually, with a teacher mentor, or with the teacher whose classroom the new teacher observed.

Notice that in a truly active classroom like the one described above, the kids do the lion's share of the work, and the teacher is far less exhausted at the end of the day. In Cindy Rickert's fifth-grade classroom, the kids monitor their own behavior. When a student gets sarcastic or otherwise gets out of line, students are empowered to raise their thumbs with their fists together, and say, "Always up!" This is a way of reminding students of what Rickert spends a good deal of time on during the first week of school: modeling and expecting a positive attitude. Notice, too, that the fifth graders in her classroom look out for each other. One of her students told me he fell on the playground during recess; his classmates rushed over, picked him up, dusted him off, and cheered for him. He told me that Rickert's class had become a family over the weeks and months. Rickert's students are constantly in motion, they love coming to school, and their grades are extremely high.

Figure 8.1 The Active Classroom

Kids standing and moving

Kids pairing and sharing

Kids transitioning from seatwork to feetwork

Kids smiling and laughing out loud

Kids charting in trios or quartets

Kids recording and reporting

Kids collaborating

Kids taking brain breaks with music and exercise

Kids managing the learning process

Kids reminding each other of what is acceptable

Kids influencing each other positively

Kids looking out for each other

Kids doing 80% of the work

and

Teachers observing and facilitating process

Contrast this, if you will, with what I admit my secondary classrooms looked like early in my teaching career (Figure 8.2). I must warn the reader that it is not for the faint of heart.

I truly believed, early in my career, that my job was to present the information; the students' job was to take notes and process the information on their own, ready to take the only kind of assessment with which I was familiar: summative quizzes and tests. When I asked a question in class, a member of my "fan club" (six or seven strong) was always available to raise a hand and provide the answer—much to my satisfaction. I now know why my energy level dropped so precipitously

Figure 8.2 Ron's (Passive) Early Classrooms

Ron standing next to the overhead

Ron writing on the overhead

Ron attached at the hip to the overhead

Ron talking, giving the students the benefit of his experience and wisdom

Ron talking to his "fan club"

Ron talking to himself on occasion

Ron "putting out fires" on more occasions

Ron getting in Eddie's face

Ron doing 80% of the work in class

Ron going home exhausted at the end of the day

Ron contemplating another line of work

and

Kids sitting passively, taking notes (then passing them), going to a better place in their minds, and going home with energy to burn

about 25 minutes or so after the students departed for home at the end of the day—that's how long it takes adrenalin to leave the body. I had been pumping adrenalin all day long in response to this problem or that fidgety student, or when Eddie discovered the location of my last nerve and stepped all over it. I did 80% of the work, and I really required little of my students during my lectures or for the length of time it took to show a video or have them complete a review worksheet. For years, I worked *much* harder than my students did.

One Last Reflection on Reflection

Experience is a natural by-product of what we do; reflection takes that experience and teaches us something that will help *improve* what we do. Jackson (2009) articulates it well: "Master teachers take the time to reflect on their teaching in order to expose unwarranted or harmful assumptions they may hold, reveal fallacies in their thinking, illuminate problems, and determine directions for new growth" (p. 3). Administrators can take the time to reflect with teachers in a large-group setting; teacher mentors can reflect with their protégés; teachers can reflect in quiet moments or with peers; and, as in the example that follows, *teachers can take the time to have students reflect on process in the classroom.*

Kelly Smith—Grade 1 Teacher

Smith understands that each time her students meet in pairs, trios, or groups, they gain experience in the art of collaboration. She also understands that if her students do not take the time to reflect on how they did when they collaborated, they will not improve. During the very first week of school, Smith and her students brainstorm a list of those qualities that good part-ners must have. During this process, she asks questions: What should a good partnership look like? (equal workload); What should it sound like? (no argu-ing). Smith and her students invest a good deal of time putting the process horse in front of the content cart. By doing this, they increase their chances of having good conversations and work sessions when content is introduced into the mix.

Students choose partners, and they practice having paired conversations—incorporating their own ideas as to what makes an effective pair or group. Once the activity is over, Smith has them answer the following questions: Were we good partners? Why, or why not? What did we do that was effective? Did we get the job done? Finally, they ask themselves the all-important question: What do we need to do next time in order to improve?

Once they have the process down, Smith introduces content. Her students now begin to work in pairs and groups to come up with answers to ques-tions, solve problems, or simply share what each of them knows about a spe-cific topic. In addition to evaluating how well they communicated and collaborated, students now begin to look at how well they know the infor-mation they were asked to discuss. Process meets content.

As Smith well understands, experience does not necessarily lead to improvement; reflection is the catalyst for progress. Allowing plenty of time for students to *reflect* on that experience can improve process and facilitate deeper understanding when it comes to content. In Smith's elementary school, teachers regularly have students self-evaluate by reflecting on "the glows" (what they did well) and "the grows" (what they could do in order to improve). Having students do this often helps build a reflective capacity into a collaborationist culture. In Smith's classroom, the kids do; they talk about what they did; they identify that which they did well; and they walk away with an understanding of what they can do to improve the next time they meet.

When administrators and teachers harness the power of reflective thought in a systemic way, then the staff has gone a long way toward building a reflective capacity into the fabric of school life. When feedback from stakeholders is a regular part of that process, the insights gained will contribute to forward progress that will benefit students and staff. When students are made part of the feedback mechanism, their perspectives will enrich improvement efforts. At all levels (building and classroom), it is critical that time be set aside for collaborative reflection. Hord and Sommers (2008) remind us, "Taking time to reflect has a cost. Not taking time to reflect has a bigger cost in terms of learning" (p. 152). Pausing to learn from experience through purposeful reflection is worth the price.

Final Thoughts

It was my own professional and personal reflections on my first 36 years in education that led me to write the *Active Classroom Series*. In the months and years that have passed since I began to write the first of these books, I have become more convinced than ever that teachers need to shift the workload to their students. As the years pass, students become less likely to want to come to school to watch teachers do the work; active teachers understand that, and they adjust their pedagogy accordingly. Kids who are kept too long in a passive state look for ways to become active; the pencil sharpener, wastebasket, and restroom become the destination of choice for students who simply have to move. Active teachers understand that, too, and they look for ways to utilize that need to move rather than fight it on a daily basis. Students are social creatures; active teachers understand that, and they look for ways to provide opportunities for discussion and other forms of verbal processing.

Active classrooms I have observed are vibrant and exciting places of learning. Kids move, pair, share, laugh, and learn in the hands of teachers who harness their students' need to move and socialize. Climbing the cognitive ladder, students in active classrooms learn to explain, illustrate, summarize, infer, analyze, synthesize, and defend a point of view. Teachers in those classrooms encourage curiosity and facilitate discovery; they use storytelling as a way to build context in such a way that their students' brains will later make the connections that lead to understanding. Active teachers build solid relationships with students, peers, and parents; they spend the first week of school perfecting process on their way to introducing content.

Most of all, I have observed first hand that active classrooms are places students *want to be*. Those kids go home and talk about what happened in school without having to be prompted. In that kind of environment, students and teachers thrive and make relentless forward progress. When students have the opportunity to think, create, give feedback, make mistakes, and safely share in a classroom of friends and learning partners—they develop the kind of confidence (collective and individual) that will serve them well down the road. Active teachers understand this; active teachers spend their time trying to do better tomorrow what they did today, all the while helping Eddie to do the same. The active classroom's continuous-improvement highway is crowded with people moving ever forward, confident that steady progress is eminently achievable—and infinitely more interesting for the teacher and her students.

Appendix A

Step-by-Step Directions for Paired Verbal Fluency (PVF)
Direction: "Stand up, and find a partner other than someone at your table." **Direction:** "Decide who will be **A** and who will be **B**." **Direction:** "**A**, raise your hand." And, "**B**, raise your hand." Then, "Hands down!" **Direction:** "Our topic for discussion is _____. **A**, when I say, 'Go!' I'll give you 60 seconds to talk about the topic. Now **B**, while **A** is talking, listen carefully. When I say, 'Switch!' **B** will begin talking about this same topic with a twist. You may not repeat anything **A** said during her 60 seconds of fame." **Direction:** "Look at the board once again to see the topic." **Direction:** "**A**, you are on . . . Go!"
Partner **A** speaks directly to Partner **B** for 60 seconds on the chosen topic.
Direction: After 60 seconds, the teacher says, "Switch!"
On the same topic, Partner **B** takes over for 60 seconds without repeating what **A** said.
Direction: After 60 seconds, the teacher says, "Stop! Look this way."
Direction: "Well done. Thank your partner for sharing. On to the next step." **Direction:** "This time, **B** will go first. As you think about the 2-minute conversation you and **A** had a few moments ago, were there some things left undiscussed, something important left out? When I say, 'Go!' you'll have 30 seconds to add whatever you think has yet to be discussed as it relates to the topic. When I say, 'Switch!' **A** will have another 30 seconds to add whatever she thinks has not been disclosed about the topic." **Direction:** "**B**, you are on . . . Go!"
On the same topic, Partner **B** goes first and adds whatever he thinks might have been left out of the initial conversation.
Direction: After 30 seconds, the teacher says, "Switch!"
On the same topic, Partner **A** adds information she thinks was left unsaid so far in the conversation.
Direction: After 30 seconds, the teacher says, "Stop! Look this way."
Direction: "One final task, and **A** will go first. When I say, 'Go!' **A** will summarize in 20 seconds or so some of the most important points made by both of you during the conversation. When I say, 'Switch!' **B** will have the opportunity to summarize any points not made by **A** in a final 20 seconds. Questions?" **Direction:** "**A**, you are on . . . Go!"
Partner **A** will summarize what was said so far.
Direction: After 20 seconds, the teacher says, "Switch!"
Partner **B** adds to the summary what **A** may have left out.
Direction: After 20 seconds, the teacher says, "Stop! Look this way."
Direction: "Thank your partner for sharing, and take your seats!"

Appendix B

Appointment Clock

Below is a full-size version of the appointment clock. Give workshop participants each a copy of this appointment clock, and instruct them to make four appointments with anyone except those in their row or at their table. Once each participant makes four appointments, he or she should be seated. If there is an odd number of participants, some may have to triple up—creating one trio—when it is time to meet and discuss something.

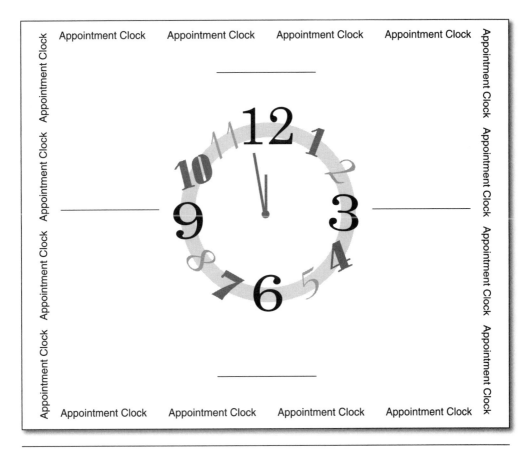

Design by Dianne Kinnison

References

Allen, R. (2008). *Green light classrooms: Teaching techniques that accelerate learning.* Thousand Oaks, CA: Corwin.

Allen, R. (2010). *High-impact teaching strategies for the 'XYZ' era of education.* Boston: Allyn & Bacon.

Bluestein, J. (2001). *Creating emotionally safe schools: A guide for educators and parents.* Deerfield Beach, FL: Health Communications.

Bluestein, J. (2008). *The win-win classroom: A fresh and positive approach to classroom management.* Thousand Oaks, CA: Corwin.

Brookhart, S. M. (2008). *How to give effective feedback to your students.* Alexandria, VA: Association for Supervision and Curriculum Development.

Brooks, J. G., & Brooks, M. G. (1999). *In search of understanding: The case for constructivist classrooms.* Alexandria, VA: Association for Supervision and Curriculum Development.

Burke, K. (2006). *From standards to rubrics in 6 steps: Tools for assessing student learning, K–8.* Thousand Oaks, CA: Corwin.

Burke, K. (2009). *How to assess authentic learning* (5th ed.). Thousand Oaks, CA: Corwin.

Costa, A. (2008). *The school as a home for the mind: Creating mindful curriculum, instruction, and dialogue.* Thousand Oaks, CA: Corwin.

Crownover, D. (1999). *Take it to the next level.* Dallas, TX: NextLevel Press.

Deci, E. (1995). *Why we do what we do: Understanding self-motivation.* New York: Penguin.

Feinstein, S. (2004). *Secrets of the teenage brain: Research-based strategies for reaching & teaching today's adolescents.* Thousand Oaks, CA: Corwin.

Fullan, M. (2010). *Motion leadership: The skinny on becoming change savvy.* Thousand Oaks, CA: Corwin.

Garmston, R. (1997). *The presenter's fieldbook: A practical guide.* Norwood, MA: Christopher-Gordon.

Garmston, R. & Wellman, B. (1999). *The adaptive school: A sourcebook for developing collaborative groups.* Norwood, MA: Christopher-Gordon.

Gregory, G., & Parry, T. (1998). *Designing brain-compatible learning.* Arlington Heights, IL: Skylight Professional Development.

Gunter, M. A., Estes, T. H., & Schwab, J. (1999). *Instruction: A models approach* (3rd ed.). Boston: Allyn & Bacon.

Hord, S. M., & Sommers, W. A. (2008). *Leading professional learning communities: Voices from research and practice.* Thousand Oaks, CA: Corwin.

Jackson, R. (2009). *Never work harder than your students & other principles of great teaching.* Alexandria, VA: Association for Supervision and Curriculum Development.

Jensen, E. (2005). *Teaching with the brain in mind* (2nd ed.). Alexandria, VA: Association for Supervision and Curriculum Development.

Jones, F. (2007). *Tools for teaching: Discipline, instruction, motivation.* Santa Cruz, CA: Fredric H. Jones & Associates.

Kaufeldt, M. (2005). *Teachers, change your bait! Brain-compatible differentiated instruction.* Bethel, CT: Crown House.

Knight, J. (2007). *Instructional coaching: A partnership approach to improving instruction.* Thousand Oaks, CA: Corwin.

Kohn, A. (1999). *The schools our children deserve: Moving beyond traditional classrooms and "tougher standards."* New York: Houghton Mifflin.

Lezotte, L. (1992). *Creating the total quality effective school.* Okemos, MI: Effective School Products.

Lipton, L., & Wellman, B. (2000). *Pathways to understanding: Patterns and practices in the learning-focused classroom* (3rd ed.). Guilford, VT: Pathways.

McGuire, F. (1998). *The power of personal storytelling: Spinning tales to connect with others.* New York: Jeremy P. Tarcher/Putnam.

Marzano, R., Pickering, D., & Pollock, J. (2001). *Classroom instruction that works: Research-based strategies for increasing student achievement.* Alexandria, VA: Association for Supervision and Curriculum Development.

Medina, J. (2008). *Brain rules: 12 principals for surviving and thriving at work, home, and school.* Seattle, WA: Pear Press.

Nash, R. (2008). *The active classroom: Practical strategies for involving students in the learning process.* Thousand Oaks, CA: Corwin.

Nash, R. (2009). *The active teacher: Practical strategies for maximizing teacher effectiveness.* Thousand Oaks, CA: Corwin.

Popham, W. J. (2008). *Transformative assessment.* Alexandria, VA: Association for Supervision and Curriculum Development.

Ratey, J. (2008). *Spark: The revolutionary new science of exercise and the brain.* New York: Little, Brown and Company.

Smith, A. (2005). *The brain's behind it: New knowledge about the brain and learning.* Norwalk, CT: Crown House.

Sousa, D. (2001). *How the brain learns.* Thousand Oaks, CA: Corwin.

Sprenger, M. (2005). *How to teach so students remember.* Alexandria, VA: Association for Supervision and Curriculum Development.

Sprenger, M. (2009). Focusing the digital brain. *Educational Leadership, 67*(1), pp. 34–39.

Tileston, D. W. (2004). *What every teacher should know about student motivation.* Thousand Oaks, CA: Corwin.

Trilling, B., & Fadel, C. (2009). *21st century skills: Learning for life in our times.* San Francisco: Jossey-Bass.

Trost, S. G., & van der Mars, H. (2009–2010). Why we should not cut P. E. *Educational Leadership, 67*(4), pp. 60–65.

Vatterott, C. (2009). *Rethinking homework: Best practices that support diverse needs.* Alexandria, VA: Association for Supervision and Curriculum Development.

Wagner, T. (2008). *The global achievement gap: Why even our best schools don't teach the new survival skills our children need—and what we can do about it.* New York: Basic Books.

Walsh, J. A., & Sattes, B. D. (2005). *Quality questioning: Research-based practice to engage every learner.* Thousand Oaks, CA: Corwin.

Wong, H. K., & Wong, R. (2005). *How to be an effective teacher: The first days of school.* Mountain View, CA: Harry K. Wong.

Index

CORWIN

A SAGE Company

The Corwin logo—a raven striding across an open book—represents the union of courage and learning. Corwin is committed to improving education for all learners by publishing books and other professional development resources for those serving the field of PreK–12 education. By providing practical, hands-on materials, Corwin continues to carry out the promise of its motto: **"Helping Educators Do Their Work Better."**